A Child's Romance

BY

PIERRE LOTI

Author of "Rarahu," etc.

TRANSLATED FROM THE FRENCH

BY

Mrs. CLARA BELL

AUTHORIZED EDITION

REVISED AND CORRECTED IN THE UNITED STATES

NEW YORK
W. S. GOTTSBERGER & CO., PUBLISHERS
11 MURRAY STREET
1891

Entered according to Act of Congress, in the year 1891
By W. S. GOTTSBERGER & CO.
in the Office of the Librarian of Congress, at Washington

This scarce antiquarian book is included in our special *Legacy Reprint Series*. In the interest of creating a more extensive selection of rare historical book reprints, we have chosen to reproduce this title even though it may possibly have occasional imperfections such as missing and blurred pages, missing text, poor pictures, markings, dark backgrounds and other reproduction issues beyond our control. Because this work is culturally important, we have made it available as a part of our commitment to protecting, preserving and promoting the world's literature. Thank you for your understanding.

TO HER MAJESTY
ELIZABETH
QUEEN OF ROUMANIA.

December, 188...

It is almost too late in my life to undertake this book; a kind of night is already closing in on me; how can I find words fresh and young enough?

I shall begin it to-morrow at sea; at least I will endeavour to put into it all that was best in me at a time when as yet there was nothing very bad.

I shall end at an early stage, in order that love may find no place in it, excepting in the form of a vague dream.

And I shall offer it to the sovereign lady who suggested the idea of writing it as the humble homage

of fascinated respect.

PIERRE LOTI.

A CHILD'S ROMANCE.

I.

IT is with a kind of fear that I approach the enigma of my impressions at the beginning of life, doubting whether indeed I felt them myself, or whether they were not, rather, remoter memories mysteriously transmitted. I feel a sort of religious reluctance to sound those depths.

On emerging from primeval night my mind did not grow gradually to the light by progressive gleams, but by sudden flashes of illumination, which abruptly dilated my childish eyes and fixed me in watchful reveries, and which then vanished, plunging me once more into the total unconsciousness of little new-born animals, of infant plants that have just begun to sprout.

At the dawn of life my history would be simply that of a much petted, much tended child, very obedient and prettily behaved, to whom nothing unforeseen could happen in its little padded world, and on whom no blow could fall that was not deadened by the tenderest solicitude.

So I make no attempt to write so tedious a tale. I will only record, without order or connection, certain moments which struck me strangely — struck me so that to this day I remember them with perfect clearness — now, when I have already forgotten so many poignant incidents, so many places, and adventures, and faces.

At that time I was a little like what a swallow might be, hatched out yesterday high up on the peak of a roof, which should begin to open its bright young eye from time to time, and fancy, as it looked down into a yard or a street, that it saw the depths of the universe and space. Thus, during these flashes of perception I furtively discerned all sorts of infinitudes of which I no doubt possessed latent conceptions in my brain, from before my individual existence; then, involuntarily closing the still-dim eye of my spirit, I sank back again for days into the original peaceful night.

At first my brain, still so new and so darkened, might have been compared to a photographic apparatus full of sensitized glasses. On these virgin plates, insufficiently illuminated objects make no impression; while if, on the contrary, a bright light, of whatever nature, falls on them, they become blotted with large light patches, on which the unknown external objects are presently engraved. — My early memories are, in fact, always full of summer sunshine, blazing noons, — or else of wood-fires with leaping red flames.

II.

I REMEMBER as though it were yesterday the evening when, after having been able to walk for some little time, I suddenly discovered the right way to jump and run, and in my excitement over this delightful novelty, went on till I tumbled down.

It must have been at the beginning of the second winter of my life, at the sad hour of nightfall. In the dining-room of our home — which at that time seemed to me immensely spacious — I had been sitting, no doubt but for a moment, subdued and quiet under the influence of the growing dusk. No lamps as yet were lighted anywhere. But the dinner hour was approaching, and a maid came in who cast an armful of brushwood on the hearth to revive the smouldering logs. Then a fine, bright fire, a sudden cheerful blaze leaped up, illuminating the whole room, and a large, round patch of light fell on the middle of the carpet, on the floor, on the rug, on the legs of the chairs, on all that lower region which was especially mine. And the flames flew up, changed, writhed and curled, every moment higher and livelier, making the long-drawn shadows dance and flicker up the wall. — I stood quite upright, full of admiration — for I remember now that I had been sitting at the feet of my grand-aunt Bertha — even then a very old woman — who was napping in her chair near a window where the grey night looked in. I was sitting on an old-fashioned foot-warmer with two steps; such a comfortable perch for a tiny coaxing child, resting its head on its grandmother's or grand-aunt's knees. — Well, I stood up in an ecstasy, and went nearer to the fire; then, within the circle of light on the carpet I began to walk round and round, to spin faster and faster, and at last, feeling suddenly in my legs an unwonted elasticity, something like the release of springs, I invented a new and most amusing exercise: this was to push very hard with my feet against the ground, then to lift up both feet at once for an instant, and to drop again, and to take advantage of the recoil to go up again — and so to go on, again and again, poof, poof! making a great deal of noise on the floor, and feeling a little pleasant giddiness. From that moment I knew how to jump, I knew how to run!

I am quite sure that it was for the first time, I remember so clearly my extreme amusement and gleeful surprise.

"Why, bless me! What has come over the

child this evening?" said my grand-aunt Bertha, somewhat uneasy. I can hear her abrupt tones now.

But still I jumped. Like the little foolish insects, drunk with light, which whirl round the lamp of an evening, I still jumped in the bright patch which spread, and shrank, and changed its shape, the borders wavering as the flames rose and fell. And all this is so present to me still that my eye recalls every line of the carpet on which it took place. It was made of a certain everlasting material woven in the neighbourhood by country weavers, and now quite out of fashion; it was called *nouis*. The house we then lived in was still as it had been arranged by my maternal grandmother when she had decided on quitting the *island* to settle on the mainland. (I shall have more to say about this *island*, which ere long assumed a mysterious charm for my baby imagination). It was a very unpretending country-house, where Huguenot austerity was plainly felt, and where immaculate cleanliness and order were the only luxuries.

Well, in the patch of light, which was now decidedly diminishing, I still jumped. But even while I jumped I was thinking with an intensity which certainly was not habitual. With my little legs, my mind too had been roused; a brighter light had been struck in my brain, where the dawn of ideas was as yet so dim. And it is, no doubt, to this mental awakening that this brief moment of my life owes its unfathomable inner side, especially the persistency with which it remains ineffaceably graven on my memory. But in vain do I endeavour to find words to express all this, while its infinite depths escape me. — There I was, looking at the chairs in a row close to the wall, and as I recollected the grown-up persons — grandmothers, grand-aunts and aunts, who commonly sat on them, who presently would come and sit on them. Why were they not there now? At this moment I longed for their presence as a protection. They were up-stairs, no doubt, in their rooms, on the second floor; between them and me there was the dark staircase — a staircase full of shadows which made me quake. — And my mother? Above all I wished for her; but she, I knew, was out in the long streets of which the ends were beyond my ken, far away and dim. I had myself seen her out of the house, asking her: "You will come back again?" And she had promised that she certainly would come back. (I have since been told that when I was quite a little child I never let any one of the family go out of the house, even for the smallest errand or call, without assuring myself of their intending to return: "You are sure you will come back?" was the question I was wont to ask anxiously, after following those who were going out, as far as the door). So my mother was out — it gave me a little tightness about the heart to know that she was out.

The streets! I was very glad that I was not out in the streets, where it was cold and dark, and where little children might be lost. It was so comfortable here in front of the warming flames — so comfortable *in my own home!* Perhaps I had never understood this as I did this evening; perhaps this was my first genuine impression of attachment to the family hearth, and of melancholy uneasiness at the thought of the vast unknown outside. It must also have been the first conscious impulse of affection for those venerable faces of aunts and grandmothers which surrounded my infancy, and which, at that hour of dusky, twilight qualms, I longed to see, all in their accustomed places, seated in a circle round me. . . . .

Meanwhile the beautiful wayward flames in the chimney seemed to be dying; the armful of small wood had burnt out, and, as the lamp was not yet lighted it was darker than before. I had already had one tumble on the carpet without hurting myself, and had begun again, more eager than ever. Now and then I found a strange delight in going into the darkest nooks where vague terrors came over me of nameless things; and then returning to safety within the circle of light, looking back with a shiver to see whether anything had come behind me out of the black corners, to follow and catch me.

Presently, the flames having quite died out, I

was really frightened; Aunt Bertha, too motionless in her chair, whose eyes I felt upon me, no longer gave me a sense of protection. The chairs even, the chairs set all round the room, began to disquiet me by their tall dancing shadows which leapt up behind them at the pleasure of the dying flare, exaggerating the height of their tall backs against the wall. And above all there was a door, half open to a dark anteroom which led to the big dining-room, yet more empty and black ... Oh! That door. I gazed at it now with a fixed stare, and nothing in the world would have made me dare to turn my back on it.

This was the beginning of the winter-evening terrors which, even in that well-beloved home, brought much gloom into my childhood.

The thing I dreaded to see had as yet no definite form; it was not till later that my visions took a shape. But my fear was not therefore the less real, and transfixed me with wide open eyes in front of the fire which no longer gave any light, — when, on a sudden, from the other side, through another door, my mother came in. Oh, how I flung myself upon her! I hid my head, I wrapped myself in her skirts. This was the supreme protection, the refuge where nothing could harm me, the nest of all nests where everything was forgotten. And from that moment the thread of my reminiscences is broken; I can follow it no further.

III.

AFTER the ineffaceable image left by that first fright, and that first dance in front of a winter's blaze, months must have passed by without leaving any mark on my brain. I had relapsed into the gloaming of life's beginnings, across which flit only wavering and confused visions — grey or rose-coloured in the hues of dawn.

I think that my next impression was one which I will try to record: an impression of summer, of broad sunshine, and of nature, and of a delicious panic at finding myself alone in the deep June grass taller than my head. But here the undercurrent is still more complicated, more mingled with things antecedent to my present existence; I feel that I must lose myself in them without succeeding in expressing anything.

It happened in a country-house called *la Limoise*, which at a later date played an important part in my child-life. It belonged to some very old friends of our family, the D***, who were our neighbours in town, their house almost touching ours. Possibly I had already been at Limoise the summer before, but at the stage of a white doll in arms. The day of which I am about to speak was certainly the first which I had spent there as a little creature capable of thought, of grief, of dreams.

I have forgotten the beginning — the departure, the journey, and the arrival. But I can see myself one very hot afternoon, see myself very happy alone in the neglected old garden, enclosed by grey walls overgrown with moss and lichen, from the woods, sandy heaths, and stony commons that surrounded it. For me, a town-bred child, this spacious garden, never kept up, where the fruit-trees were perishing of old age, was as full of surprises and mysteries as the virgin forest. Having, no doubt, stepped over a high box edging, I had lost myself in the middle of one of the uncultured beds far from the house, among I know not what wayward growths — asparagus run to seed I daresay — tangled with wild creepers. There I had squatted down after the manner of little children, to bury myself in all this, which was far above my head even when I stood up. And I kept very still, with eyes dilated and my mind attent, at once alarmed and delighted. What I felt in the presence of these new things was, even then, less astonishment than remembrance; that lavish greenery which closed in upon me I *knew* was everywhere, in the remotest depths of the unseen country. I felt it all about me, melancholy, immense, vaguely apprehended already. It frightened and yet it attracted me — and in order to stay there as long as possible without being sought out, I hid myself more completely, with the look on my face, no doubt of a little Red-skin in glee at finding his forest again.

But suddenly I heard myself called: "Pierre! Pierre! My little Pierrot!" And without replying I made haste to lie down flat on the earth under the weeds and the finely cut leaves of the fennel-like asparagus branches.

Again: "Pierre! Pierre!" — It was Lucette. I knew her voice, and I even understood from her laughing tone that she spied me in my green lurking-place. But I could not see her. I looked about on all sides, in vain. No one! Still she called me with shouts of laughter, her voice more and more full of fun. Where in the world could she be?

Ah! Up there, high in the air, perched in the fork of a strangely twisted tree, which had what looked like a hoary head of lichen.

Then I got up, greatly disgusted at having been thus discovered. And as I rose I perceived from afar, above the tangle of wild plants, a corner of the old ivy-crowned walls, which surrounded the garden. Those walls were to become very familiar to me as time went on, for during my half-holidays from school I have spent many an hour perched at the top, looking out over the peaceful pastoral landscape, dreaming, to the chirp of the grasshoppers, of yet more sunny spots in distant lands. And on that particular day their mortarless grey stones, scorching in the sun and blotted with patches of lichen, gave me for the first time in my life an undefined impression of the oldness of things, a vague conception of stretches of time before my life, — of the Past.

Lucette D***, older than I by eight or ten years, was in my eyes almost a grown-up person. I could not have known her long, but I had known her as long as I could know anything. After this I loved her as a sister; and then her early death was one of my first real griefs as a little boy.

This is my first recollection of her — an apparition among the boughs of an old apple-tree. And even that has held its ground merely by the association of the two new feelings with which it was mingled: a fascinated uneasiness in the presence of the invading greenery of Nature, and a dreamy regretfulness as I looked at the old walls, for old things, and a bygone time.

IV.

I SHOULD now like to try to describe the impression made on me by the sea on the occasion of our first interview — which was a short and dreary tête-à-tête.

This impression, as an exception — was a twilight effect; it was almost too dark to see, and yet the image, as it appeared to me, was so intense as to remain stamped at one blow and for ever. And to this day I feel a retrospective thrill when I concentrate my mind on this remembrance.

I had arrived late in the day, with my parents, at a village on the coast of Saintonge, at a fisherman's cottage let for the bathing season. I knew that we had come for what was called the sea, but I had not yet seen it; a ridge of sand-hills hid it from me by reason of my being so small — and I was in a state of great impatience to make its acquaintance. So after dinner, as it was growing dusk, I slipped out alone. The sharp briny air had a smell of something unknown, and a strange sound, low but immense, was audible behind the little humps of sand to which a path led.

Everything was fearsome to me — the bit of unknown path, the twilight under a cloudy sky, and the very solitude of this corner of a village. However, strong in one of those sudden resolutions which the most timid creatures sometimes form, I set out with a firm step.

Then suddenly I stood still, rigid and shivering with terror. In front of me lay something — something dark and sounding, which had risen up on all sides at once and seemed to be without end; a spread of motion which gave me a deadly sense of giddiness. *That was it*, evidently; not an instant of doubt, nor even of surprise at its being like this; no, nothing but awe; I recognized it and trembled. It was of an obscure green, almost black; it looked unstable, treacherous, greedy; it was seething and raving everywhere at once with sinister malignity. Above it stretched the sky in unbroken leaden-grey, like a heavy cloak.

Very far, and only very far away, in the unmeasurable depths of the horizon there was a rent, a slit between the clouds and the waters, a long vacant rift of dim yellow pallor.

Now to recognize the sea, as I did, had I seen it before? — Perhaps, unconsciously, in the island when, at the age of five or six months I had been taken to see a grand-aunt, my grandmother's sister. Or had it been so often gazed at by my sailor ancestors that I was born with some confused reflection in my mind of its vast expanse.

We remained face to face a moment — I, fascinated by the sight. From that very first interview, no doubt, I had an undefinable presentiment that the sea would at length some day take possession of me, in spite of all my hesitancy, in spite of all the wills which would combine to withhold me. What I felt in its presence was not simple dread, but above all a nameless melancholy, a sense of desolate solitude, desertion and exile. And I turned away, running with my face very much puckered up I should suppose, and my hair tossed by the wind, in the greatest haste to be with my mother again, to throw my arms round her and cling to her; to be comforted for a thousand coming and unutterable woes which had wrung my heart at the sight of those vast green depths.

V.

MY mother. — In the course of these notes I have already incidentally mentioned her name twice or thrice, but without dwelling on it. — At first, as it seems, she was no more to me than the natural refuge, the sanctuary from all the terrors of the unknown, all the black troubles which had no definite cause. But I think that the very earliest moment at which her image was stamped on my mind as very living and real, in a glory of true and ineffable tenderness, was one morning in the month of May when she came into my room, followed by a beam of sunshine, and bringing me a bunch of pink hyacinths. I was recovering from some childish ailment — measles, or whooping-cough, or something of the kind. — I had been condemned to stay in bed, to keep very warm, and as by the streaks of light which crept in through my shuttered windows I could guess the revived splendour of the sun and air, I was very forlorn inside the curtains of my white bed; I wanted to get up, to go out; above all to see my mother, my mother at any cost.

The door opened and my mother came in smiling. Oh! I can see her now as I saw her then in the doorway, bringing with her some of the sunshine and breeze from without. It is all before me: the expression of her eyes as they looked into mine, the sound of her voice, the very details of her beloved, familiar dress which now-a-days would look so old-world. She had come in from some morning errand in the town. She wore a straw bonnet with yellow roses and a lilac *barège* shawl — it was in the time of shawls — printed with little bunches of flowers in a darker shade. Her black curls — those poor, dear curls, which have not altered in style, but now, alas! are thinner and quite white — were then unstreaked by a thread of silver. There was a fragrance about her of sunshine and summer which she had caught out of doors. Her face that morning, framed in a bonnet with a deep *curtain* as it was called, is vividly before my eyes.

Besides the bunch of pink hyacinths she also brought me a little doll's jug and basin, exactly copied in miniature from the flowered earthenware which the country people use.

She bent over my bed to kiss me, and then I wanted nothing more — not to cry, not to get up, not to go out; she was there and that was enough; I was entirely comforted, soothed, transformed, by her beneficent presence.

I must have been a little more than three

years old at that time, and my mother about forty-two. But I had not the smallest idea of my mother's age; it never entered my head to wonder whether she were young or old; it was not indeed till somewhat later that I discovered that she was very pretty. No; at that time it was She, and that was all; as much as to say that the face was to me unique, — never to be compared with any other — from which there beamed on me joy, safety, and tenderness, from which all good emanated, including infant faith and prayer.

On this first appearance in my book of memories, of that thrice blessed face, I would fain, if it were possible, greet it with words made on purpose for her, such as indeed do not exist; words which of themselves should make tears of healing flow, and should have I know not what sweetness of consolation and forgiveness; which should include, too, a persistent hope, unfailing and invincible, of an eternal reunion in Heaven. For, since I have touched on this mystery and this illogical vein in my mind, I will here say, by the way, that my mother is the only living soul from whom I do not feel that death will divide me for ever. With other human beings whom I have loved with all the powers of my heart and soul, I have tried passionately to imagine any kind of hereafter, a morrow somewhere else, a something — I know not what — immaterial and everlasting; but no — nothing — I cannot; I have always had a horrible consciousness of abysmal nothingness, very dust of very dust.

But with regard to my mother I have preserved my early beliefs almost intact. Still, meseems that when I shall have done with playing my poor little part in this world, have done with seeking the impossible over endless unbeaten tracks, have done with amusing other folks by my fatigues and torments, I shall go to rest somewhere, welcomed by my mother who will have led the way; and the smile of serene assurance which she now wears will then have become a smile of triumphant knowledge. I do not, to be sure, very clearly see that dim Somewhere; it looms before me pale and grey, and words, however vague and indefinite they may be, give too precise a form to the dreamlike vision. And even there — I know how childish what I am going to say must be — even there I picture my mother under her present earthly aspect, with her dear grey curls, and the fine lines of her pretty profile, which years are gradually defacing but which I still admire. The thought that my mother's face may some day vanish for ever from my sight, that it can be no more than a combination of elements liable to disintegration and to be lost beyond recovery in the universal void — this thought not only makes my heart bleed, but shocks me, as a thing inconceivable and monstrous. Ah! no. I feel that there is something exceptional in that face which Death cannot touch. And my love for my mother, which has been the only unchanging love of my life, is altogether so free from every material tie that it alone is almost enough to give me confidence in one indestructible thing, namely the soul; and gives me at times a sort of inexplicable forlorn hope.

I cannot quite understand why this appearance of my mother by the side of my little sick-bed that morning should have struck me so much as she was constantly with me. Here again there is a very mysterious underside; it is as though she had at that particular moment been revealed to me for the first time in my life.

And why, among the toys I have cherished, has that little doll's jug acquired, without any will of mine, a special value, and the importance of a relic? To such a degree that when far away, at sea, and in moments of danger, I have thought of it with pathetic affection, and pictured it in the place where it has stood for years among other fragmentary treasures in a certain cupboard, never opened; to such a degree that if it were to disappear I should have lost an amulet for which nothing could be a substitute. That old lilac shawl too, which I recognized not long since among a heap of old clothes set aside to be given to the poor, — why did I have it rescued as a precious possession? In its hue, now faded, in its quaint old-fashioned flowers of Indian design, I still find tender protection and a smile; I even believe that I find soothing in it, sweet confidence, almost faith; it exhales a perfect emanation of my mother, mingling perhaps with fond regret for the May mornings of yore, which were brighter than those of to-day.

Really I am afraid this book will be terribly dull to a great many people — and there is more in it of myself than I have ever yet written.

As I write it, in the calm night-watches which are so favourable to memories, the exquisite Queen to whom I desire to dedicate it is always present to my thoughts; it is like a long letter written to her in the certainty of being understood to the very end and even beyond it, in those depths for which there are no words.

And perhaps, too, I shall be understood by unknown friends who follow me with kind but distant sympathy. For, indeed, no man who loves, or has loved, his mother, will smile at the childish things I have just said, I am quite sure.

Only to some, to whom such a love is unknown, this chapter will no doubt appear ridiculous. But those cannot conceive of the scorn I have for them in return for their shrugs.

VI.

TO end this enumeration of the confused pictures surviving from my earliest infancy I must here again speak of a sunbeam — a sad one this time — which has left its ineffaceable traces on me, and of which the sense will never be interpreted.

It was on returning from divine service one Sunday that this sunbeam fell on me. It came in on the staircase through a window set ajar, and lay in a strange patch of light on the whiteness of a wall. I had come home from church* alone with my mother, and mounted the stairs holding her hand; the silent house had the resonance peculiar to very hot summer noons — it must have been in August or September — and, as is the custom in our part of the world, the half-closed outside shutters made twilight during the hours of fierce sunshine.

* *Du Temple*. Meaning a French protestant church.

The instant I entered the house I had a gloomy sense of the Sabbath rest which, in country places, and quiet out-of-the-way ends of small towns, is like arrested vitality; but when I saw the shaft of light which shot obliquely across the stairs from the window, the pang of sadness was far more keen; something quite incomprehensible and altogether new, with an innate notion, perhaps, of the brevity of the summers of life, of their swift flight, and of the eternal indifference of their suns. But other and more mysterious elements were mingled with it which it would be impossible to suggest however vaguely.

And to this history of the sunbeam I will only add a sequel which is to me closely bound up with it. Years and years had passed by: I had become a man, had seen the uttermost ends of the earth, and known every kind of adventure, when, as it fell, I spent an autumn and winter in a solitary house in a suburb of Stamboul. There, on the wall of my staircase, every evening at the same hour, a sunbeam, falling through a window,

A CHILD'S ROMANCE. 29

lay aslant; it lighted up a sort of niche hollowed in the wall, in which I had placed an Athenian amphora. Well, I never saw that sunbeam without remembering the other, the Sunday sun of my childhood, or without feeling the same — precisely the same — impression of sadness, hardly weakened by time, and as full of mystery as ever. Then, when the time came for me to leave Turkey, to leave that dangerous little house at Stamboul which I had loved, added to all the pangs of departing there was this strange regret: that never again should I see the slanting sun fall obliquely across the stairs to rest on the niche and the Greek jar.

Beneath all this there must evidently be, if not reminiscences of personal pre-existence, at any rate some incoherent reproduction of the thoughts of ancestors — things which I am unable to resuscitate from their darkness and dust. — In short, I see, I know no more. I have got back into the domain of dreams which evade me, of vapours blown away, of the intangible nothing.

And all this chapter, almost unintelligible as

it is, has no excuse but that it has been written with a great effort at sincerity, and absolute truthfulness.

VII.

SPRING-TIME in the fresh glories of May on a lonely road known as the Fountains road. — I have tried to arrange these memories to some extent in order of dates; I may have been five by this time. Old enough therefore to walk out with my father and sister; and there I was, one dewy morning, in rapture at seeing everything become so green, the leaves growing so broad, the shrubs so bushy. By the side of the paths the plants, all coming up together, like a huge bouquet sprouting all at once from the whole earth, had blossomed out in a delicious tangle of pink herb-robert and blue speedwell; and I pulled them and pulled more, not knowing which to run to, trampling on them, wetting my legs with dew, amazed at the wealth at my feet, longing to pluck handfuls and carry all away. My sister, who held a bough of hawthorn, and flags, and tall grasses like aigrettes, bent down and taking my hand led me off, saying: " Come, that is enough for once; we could never gather them all, you see." But I paid no heed, positively intoxicated by the magnificence before me, and not remembering ever having seen the like.

This was not the first of those walks with my father and sister, which for a long time — till the dismal days of copy-books, lessons and tasks — recurred almost every day, so that I very soon knew every road in the neighbourhood and the varieties of flowers to be gathered there.

Those infertile tracts of my native province, monotonous but none the less dear; monotonous, level, uniform; meadows of hay and ox-eye daisies — where, in those days, I could be lost, disappearing among the green stems; and cornfields, and lanes hedged with hawthorn. Out to the west, on the furthest horizon, I would gaze in search of the sea which sometimes, when we had walked a long way, could be seen above the flat line of the coast, a tiny strip of blue, more absolutely level — and dragging me to itself slowly, slowly, like a huge patient lodestone, sure of its power and able to wait.

My sister, and my brother whom I have not yet mentioned, were many years older than I, so that it seemed — especially in those early days — as though I were of a later generation.

So they, too, were there to spoil me, besides my father and mother, my grandmothers, aunts and grand-aunts. And I, the only child among them all, shot up like a shrub too well cared for in a greenhouse, too much sheltered, too ignorant of the copse and thorn-brake.

VIII.

IT has been suggested that those persons who are most gifted with the power of painting — whether with colours or with words — are perhaps in a way, purblind, living habitually in a dim light, a lunar fog, their gaze turned inwards; and that therefore, when by good-hap they see, they are impressed ten times more vividly than other men.

This strikes me as a paradox. Still, it is certain that a dim light predisposes us to see better; as, in a panorama show, the darkened vestibule prepares the eye for the final triumph of illusion.

In the course of my life, therefore, I should, I daresay, have been less strongly impressed by the changeful phantasmagoria of the world, if I had not begun the journey among almost colourless surroundings, in the quietest corner of the most humdrum little town, receiving an austerely religious education, and my longest travels limited to the woods of *la Limoise* — to me as unexplored as the primeval forest — or the strand of the *island* where some notion of immensity was spread before my eyes, when I paid a visit to my old aunts at Saint-Pierre d'Oleron.

It was in the back garden of our own house

that I spent the brightest of my summers. That seemed to me my special domain and I delighted in it.

Really very pretty was that pleasance; more sunny and airy, and flowery than most town-gardens. There was a sort of long avenue of green branches and flowers, shut in on the south by a low old wall over-garlanded with roses and honeysuckles, with the tops of fruit-trees in the neighbouring gardens showing above it; a long, flowery alley, with an illusory effect of great extent, in perspective under trellices of vine and jasmine to a corner where it opened out like a large bowery room, to end at a cellar house of very ancient masonry, the grey stones hidden under creepers and ivy.

Oh! how I loved that garden; how I love it still!

The deepest and earliest memories I have kept of it are those, I think, of the fine long summer evenings. To come home from a walk in the evening, in the warm transparent twilights — which were certainly more exquisite then than they are now; to come into that back-plot filled with the sweetest odours of datura and honeysuckle, and to see from the gate the long ranks of drooping boughs! Below the first arbour, pleached with Virginian jasmine, a gap in the greenery admitted a still-luminous patch of western red. And far away at the other end, among the darkened masses of foliage, three or four persons were seen, quietly seated on chairs; in black gowns, to be sure, and motionless; but, even so, comfortable to behold, well known and well beloved: mother, grandmother, aunts. Then I set out to run and fling myself on their knees, — and that was one of the most amusing incidents of my day.

IX.

TWO children, quite little children, sitting very close together on low stools, in a large room where the shades were gathering as dusk fell in the month of March. Two little things of five or six, in short drawers and blouses, and white pinafores over them, in the fashion of that day; very quiet now — after playing the very mischief — and amusing themselves in a corner with pencils and scraps of paper, only a little uneasy with vague alarm at the waning light.

Of these two babies only one was drawing — that was I. The other, asked to spend the day as a rare treat, watched my work, getting as near as he could. With some difficulty, but full of confidence, he followed the vagaries of my pencil which I took care to explain as I went on. And explanation was in fact necessary, for I was executing two sentimental subjects which I entitled: *The Happy Duck* and *the Unhappy Duck.*

The room in which we were may have been furnished in 1805, when the poor, very old grandmother who still dwelt there, had been married; that evening she sat there in her arm-chair of the style of the *Directoire,* singing to herself, and paying no heed to us.

I remember this grandmother but vaguely, for she died but a short while after this. And as her living image will not come before us again in the course of these notes, I will devote a paragraph to her here.

Long ago, it would seem, through many trials, she had been a brave and admirable mother. After such reverses as people experienced in those days, having lost her husband at the battle of Trafalgar and her eldest son in the wreck of the *Medusa*, she had resolutely set to work to bring up her second son — my father — till the time when he, in return could surround her with kindness and comfort. When she was nearly eighty years old — and she was not far from it when I was born — senile childishness had suddenly destroyed her intellect; I therefore, never knew her otherwise than bereft of ideas — her soul absent. She would stand for a long time in front of a certain mirror, conversing in the friendliest way with her own reflection which she addressed as "my good neighbour," or "my worthy friend." But her chief craze was to sing with immense enthusiasm, the *Marseillaise*, the *Parisienne*, the *Chant du Départ* — all the great revolutionary hymns which, when she was young, had fired France; and yet, all through those stirring times she had kept very calm, thinking only of her household cares and of her boy — and it was all the more strange to hear this belated echo of the great upheaval aroused in her brain now that the dark mystery of final disorganization had begun in her. It always amused me to hear her; sometimes it made me laugh, but with no irreverent mockery; and she never frightened me because she was still so pretty; — positively pretty, with fine, regular features, a very sweet look, beautiful hair hardly streaked with white, and in her cheeks that delicate dried-rose pink which the old people of her generation were privileged to preserve. There was I know not what atmosphere of modesty, reserve, and simple virtue about her still-neat little person, which I can see as I write — generally wrapped in a red cashmere shawl, and crowned with an old-world cap trimmed with large bows of green ribbon.

Her room, where I loved to play because it was spacious and the sun shone in all the year round, was stamped with the simplicity of a country manse: furniture in black walnut wood from the time of the *Directoire*, the huge bed hung with thick red cotton twill, the walls coloured with yellow ochre and graced with water-colour drawings of vases and bunches of flowers, in tarnished gilt frames. At a very early age I fully appreciated how humble and old-fashioned the fittings of this room were; I even said to myself that this grandmamma must be much poorer than my other grandmamma, who was younger by twenty years, and always dressed in black, a much more imposing personage.

Now, to return to my two compositions in black and white, the first certainly that I had ever committed to paper: the two ducks, occupying such dissimilar social positions.

For the *Happy Duck* I had sketched in the background a little house, and near the bird a sturdy female figure calling it to be fed. The *Unhappy Duck*, on the contrary, was all alone, swimming forlorn on a sort of dim ocean suggested by two or three parallel lines, and in the distance a deserted shore. The paper was thin, a sheet torn out of some book perhaps, and printed on one side; and the letters and lines showed through in grey spots which suddenly produced the effect to my eyes of clouds in the sky. The little scrawl, more formless than a school-boy's smudge on the class-room wall, was strangely filled in by the stains in the background, and on a sudden assumed a terrible depth of meaning; in the growing twilight it spread like a vision; hollows seemed to form in the distance, like the pale undulations of the sea. I was overwhelmed by my own work, finding in it things which I had certainly not put there, and which in fact I could scarcely know. . . .

"Oh!" I cried, in great excitement, to my little playfellow, who did not understand at all, "Oh! do you know — I cannot bear to look at it." And I hid the drawing under my fingers. But I came back to it again and looked at it, on the contrary, so attentively that to this day I can see it as I saw it then, transfigured: a gleam of light lay across the horizon of that ill-drawn sea, the rest of the sky was heavy with rain, and to me it represented a winter evening in a gale. The *Unhappy Duck*, alone, far from his family and friends, was making his way, no doubt to find shelter for the night, towards the hazy shore beyond, dark with desolate gloom. And I am quite sure that for a fleeting moment I had a complete foreknowledge of those heartachings which I was to know afterwards in the course of my seafaring life, when, in foul December weather, my barque should put in at dusk, for shelter till the morrow, in some uninhabited creek on the coast of Brittany; or — and yet more — in the twilight of the southern winter, by the lands of Magellan, when we should seek a little protection for the night in those unknown regions — lands as inhospitable, as infinitely desert, as the ocean around them.

When this sort of vision was past, I found myself once more, in the great bare room shrouded in shade where my grandmother sat singing, a tiny creature who had seen nothing as yet of the wide world, frightened without knowing of what, and not even understanding how it was he had begun to cry.

Since then I have noticed that the rudimentary scrawls done by children, with their crude, false colouring, may be more striking than clever or beautiful paintings, for the very reason that they are incomplete, and that as we look at them we are led to add our own ideas — a thousand things, surging up from the unsounded depths, which no brush could ever depict.

X.

JUST above the poor old grandmother who sang the *Marseillaise*, on the second floor, and on the side of the house which looked onto courtyards and gardens, dwelt my grand-aunt Bertha. From her windows, across some buildings and low walls covered with roses and jasmine, the ramparts of the town were visible at no great distance, with their ancestral trees, and beyond them a glimpse of the wide plains of our province *prées* as they are called (sea meadows) covered in summer by tall weeds and grass, and as monotonous and level as the sea itself.

From up there the river, too, might be seen. At high tide, when it was full to the brim, it showed like a silver braid winding between the meadow-lands, and the boats, large and small, made their way in the distance along the narrow thread of water up to the port or down to the open. This was, in fact, the only view we had of the real country, and so my Aunt Bertha's window had a particular attraction for me at a very tender age. In the evening especially, at the hour of sunset, when I could see from thence the orange disk so mysteriously swallowed up behind the fields. Oh! those sunsets, seen from Aunt Bertha's windows; what rapture and what melancholy they sometimes left in my mind! — Winter sunsets, pale and rosy, through the closed pane — summer sunsets on stormy evenings blazing and gorgeous, which I could watch till the very end with every window open, breathing the odours of jasmine on the walls. Ah, no! there are no such sunsets now. When one promised to be especially splendid or weird, if I were not there, Aunt Bertha, who never missed them, would hasten to call me: "Little one, little one — come quick!" From one end of the house to the other I heard and understood her call; then I flew up as fast as I could pelt — all the faster because the staircase was beginning to be gloomy, and already at each turn I fancied imaginary forms of ghosts or monsters, who rarely failed to run after me up and down stairs at night, to my great terror.

Aunt Bertha's room, too, was humbly furnished, with white muslin curtains. The walls, papered with an old-fashioned hanging of the beginning of the century, were decorated with water-colours like grandmamma's below. But what I chiefly gazed at was a picture in crayon, copied from Raphael, of a virgin draped in white, blue and rose-colour. The last sunbeams always lighted it up — and, as I have said, the sunset hour was the hour for that room. Now this virgin was like Aunt Bertha; in spite of the great difference in their ages the resemblance of the pure, regular lines of the two profiles was quite striking.

On this same floor, but facing the street, my other grandmother lived; she who always wore black, with her daughter, my Aunt Claire, the person in all the house who did most to spoil me. I was in the habit, in the winter, of paying them a visit on leaving Aunt Bertha when the sun had gone to bed. In my grandmother's room, where I generally found these two together, I sat down by the fire on a little chair placed there for my benefit, to spend the always anxious and alarming hour of "blind man's holiday." After the movement and jumping of the day that dim hour almost always reduced me to stillness on this little chair, wide-eyed and uneasy, watching the slightest change in the outlines of the shadows, especially on the side where the door stood ajar to the darkening staircase. No doubt, if any one had known the melancholy and terrors which twilight brought me, the house would at once have been lighted to spare me; but no one understood it, and the persons about me, most of them advanced in life, were accustomed as dusk fell to remain quiet in their places for a long time without feeling the need of a lamp. As the shades grew blacker one or another — grandmother or aunt — had to bring her chair forward, nearer, very near, that I might feel her protection close behind me; then, quite safe and happy, I would say : " Now tell me a story of the Island."

" The Island" was the Island of Oleron, my mother's birthplace and theirs, which they had all three left twenty years before I was born to settle here on the mainland. And the charm which that island, and the smallest things which had come from thence, always had for me, was very singular.

We were not very far from it, for, from a certain dormer in our roof, it could be discerned in fine weather, far away beyond the level fields; a low blue line raised above that paler narrow line which was the inlet dividing it from us. But to get there was quite a journey by reason of the wretched country coaches, and the sail-boats in which we must cross, often in a stiff westerly breeze. At that time I had three old aunts living in the little town of Saint-Pierre d'Oleron, very quietly on the income from their salt marshes — the remains of scattered fortunes — and on the yearly dues paid them by the peasantry in sacks of corn. When we went to see them at Saint-Pierre, it was joy for me, mingled with a variety of complicated emotions which I could not as yet unravel completely. The predominant impression was that they themselves, their way of living, their house, their furniture, everything belonging to them, dated from a remote past, another century; and then there was the sea which I felt all round me, isolating us; the land even flatter and more wind-swept than at home; wide sands and endless shores.

My nurse, too, was a native of Saint-Pierre, of a Huguenot family devoted to ours from father to son, and she had a way of saying: "in the island" which infused into me, with a cold chill all her instinctive home-sickness.

A quantity of little objects brought from "the

island" and quite peculiar to it, had found a place in our house. First of all there were the large beach pebbles, picked out from the myriads on the ocean shore, rolled and ground for ages on the strand. These had a regular place in the domestic economy of the winter evenings; they were piled on the hearth where the great log-fires were blazing; then they were tied up in flowered chintz bags, from the island too, and placed in the beds where they kept the sleepers' feet warm till morning. And in the garden cellar there were pitch-forks and huge jars; especially there were a number of tall straight poles of elm for hanging out the washing; these were young saplings chosen and cut in my grandmother's wood. And all these things had a particular aroma of mystery to me.

I knew that my grandmother owned those woods no longer, nor her salt marshes, nor her vineyards; I had heard that she had made up her mind to sell them by degrees and to invest her money on the mainland, and that a certain dishonourable lawyer had by investing it badly reduced her possessions to a very small sum. So when I went to the island, and when certain old brine boilers, or old vine-dressers who had served the family, a faithful and submissive race, still called me *"notre petit bourgeois"* (our little squire would represent the idea) it was out of pure politeness and the deference of remembrance. But I already regretted that past. A life spent in superintending vintages and crops, which had been that of many of my forefathers, seemed to me so much more desirable than my own, shut up in a town-house.

The stories of the island, which my mother and my Aunt Claire used to tell me were stories of their childhood; and that childhood seemed to me so long, long ago, lost in ages which I could only conceive of as in the half-light of dreams. Grandparents always figured in them, grand-uncles whom I had never known, dead long years since, whose names I would have repeated, and whose aspect mystified and plunged me into endless dreaming. There was especially a certain uncle Samuel who had lived in the days of religious persecutions, and in whom I felt a very particular interest.

I did not care for variety in these stories; often indeed I would ask for one which had captivated me to be repeated.

In general they were tales of travels — on the little donkeys which used to play so important a part in the lives of the good people who inhabited the island — to visit a distant vineyard or to cross the sands of the *grande côte* — the ocean shore; and then of some terrible storm in the evening of such an excursion, compelling them to take shelter for the night in an inn or a farm.

And when my imagination was on the stretch towards all these bygone things, in the darkness which I had ceased to be aware of, "Ding-a-ding, ding-a-ding!" The dinner-bell. — I would jump up skipping for glee. We all went down together into the dining-room where I began by throwing myself against my mother and hiding my face in her dress.

XI.

GASPARD: a stumpy, clumsy little dog, by no means a beauty, but whose whole soul beamed in two large eyes full of life and good-fellowship. I have quite forgotten how he came to have been made at home with us, but he spent some months with us, and I loved him dearly.

Now one evening, during a winter's walk, Gaspard had deserted me. I was comforted by being told that he would certainly find his way back by himself, and I came home in fairly good spirits. But when it became dusk my heart grew very full.

My parents had to dine with them that evening a violin player of great talent, and I had been allowed to sit up late to hear him play. At the first strokes of his bow, as soon as he began to make some heart-broken adagio wail on the strings, it was to me as though he had evoked a vision of all the dark paths in the forest, of the black night in which creatures feel abandoned and lost; then I quite distinctly saw Gaspard wandering through the rain round a dismal spot where several ways met, and, unable to find the right one, set off towards some unknown point, never to return. — The tears came; and as no one perceived them, the violin went on, casting its mournful appeals on the silence and finding their response in the depths of the nether abyss, in visions which had no shape, no name, no meaning.

This was my first introduction to music, conjuring up shades. After this years went by before I understood anything more about it, for the little piano-forte pieces which I began to play myself — "remarkably well for my age," as I heard said — were as yet no more than a pleasant, measured sound to my ears.

XII.

THIS, now, is the story of an acute pain, produced by a book which was read to me. I never read to myself and utterly disdained books.

A very naughty little boy having left his family and his country, came back alone some years after when his parents and his sister were dead. This took place in November, of course, and the author described the grey sky and the wind which shook the last leaves off the trees.

In the deserted garden, under an arbour of bare boughs the prodigal son, stooping to the dank earth, recognized among all these autumn leaves a blue bead left there from the time when he had come there to play with his sister. — But here I started up, and bid the reader cease, feeling the sobs rising. I had seen it, literally seen the lonely garden, the old arbour stripped of its greenery, and half-hidden among the withered leaves that blue bead, a relic of the lost sister.

It all hurt me, fearfully, giving me a sense of the languishing end of existence, a feeling of the slow fading and dropping of everything.

It is strange that a childhood so tenderly sheltered should have bequeathed me chiefly images of sorrow.

Of course such sorrows were rare exceptions, and I usually lived in the gay heedlessness of all children; but no doubt these days of entire contentment, simply because they were the rule, left no trace in my brain and I find them no more.

I have also a quantity of summer memories lying like broad flecks of sunshine above the confusion of remembrance crowded into my head. And always the great heat, the deep blue skies, the twinkling sparkles in our shore of sand, the reflected blaze of light from the white walls of the cottages in the little hamlets on "the island," left an impression on my mind of melancholy and torpor such as I found again, only greatly intensified, in the lands of Islam.

XIII.

"AND at midnight there was a cry made: 'Behold the bridegroom cometh; go ye out to meet him.' And the virgins which were ready went in with him to the marriage: and the door was shut. Then came also the foolish virgins saying: 'Lord, Lord, open unto us!' But he answered and said: 'Verily I say unto you, I know you not.' Watch, therefore, for ye know neither the day nor the hour wherein the Son of man cometh."

After reading these verses aloud, my father closed the Bible; there was pushing of chairs in the drawing-room where we all were collected, including the servants, and every one knelt down to pray. This was the rule every evening, after the manner of the old Protestant families — just before separating for the night.

"The door was shut." I, on my knees, was

not following the prayer, for the foolish virgins appeared to me. They were robed in white veils which floated behind them in their eager haste, and they had little lamps in their hands with quivering flames which immediately went out and left them in the outer darkness before that closed door, irrevocably shut to all eternity. — Then a moment might come when it would be too late to entreat, when the Lord, weary of our sinning, would no longer hearken! I had never before thought of this as possible. And deep and gloomy fear, which nothing in my baby faith had ever caused me till this day, took possession of me at the notion of irrevocable damnation.

For a long, long time, for weeks and months, the parable of the foolish virgins haunted my dreams. And every evening, as the dusk fell, I repeated to myself the no less awful than comforting words: "Watch therefore, for ye know neither the day nor the hour wherein the Son of man cometh." — "If he were to come to-night," thought I, "if I were to be aroused by the noise of many waters, by the angel's trump sounding the terrific signal for the end of the world." And I could not go to sleep till I had said my prayers at great length and besought the mercy of the Lord.

Nor do I believe that any small creature ever had a more timid conscience than I; over every little thing I was tormented with scruples which those who loved me best often failed to understand, and which made my heart very full. I remember, for instance being miserable for days together out of some fear of having said something, or told some tale which was not absolutely accurate. To such a point that almost always when I had told my story or made my statement I was heard to murmur in an undertone, as if I were telling my beads: "After all, perhaps I do not exactly know how it all was." Even now I look back with retrospective oppression on the thousand little fits of remorse and fear of sin which, from my sixth to my eighth year, cast a chill, a shadow, on my childhood.

At that time if I ever was asked what I meant to be as I grew up, I unhesitatingly answered: "A minister," and my religious vocation seemed great and genuine. Those about me would smile, no doubt thinking it well since I wished it.

In the evening, and more especially at night, I was always thinking of that *hereafter* which I already knew by the awful name of Eternity. And my exit from this world — a world as yet scarce seen in one of its most colourless and forgotten spots — seemed to me a very near thing. It was with mingled feelings of impatience and mortal terror that I pictured myself as very soon to wear a robe of shining white, in the glory of the Great Light, sitting with the throng of angels and the elect round "the Throne of the Lamb" in a vast unstable circle which would oscillate slowly but continuously, in vertiginous motion, to the sound of music in the infinite void of heaven.

XIV.

"ONCE upon a time a little girl, opening a great big fruit from the colonies, there came out a beast — a green beast — which stung her — and she died of it."

It was my little friend Antoinette — she six and I seven — who told me this story, apropos to an apricot which we had just divided.

We are sitting at the bottom of her garden, in the sweet month of June, under a thick apricot-tree, close together on one stool in a hut as big as a bee-hive, built with our own hands for our private accommodation, out of old planks, covered with West Indian matting which had served to pack coffee imported from the Antilles. Tiny specks of sunlight peep through our roof of coarse woven reeds, and dance on our white pinafores and our faces, broken by the leaves of the trees which are stirred by a warm breeze.

For at least two summers our favourite amusement was building these Robinson Crusoe huts in corners which we fancied solitary, and sitting in them quite hidden to hold our chat. In the story of the little girl stung by a beast these words alone had plunged me at once into a reverie: "A great big fruit from the colonies." And a vision had come to me of trees, and strange fruits, and forests peopled with wonderful birds.

Ah! how full of emotion and magic to my childhood was that single word "the colonies," which at that time meant to me the whole region of the distant tropics, with their palms, their huge flowers, their negroes, their animals, their adventures. From the confusion of my notions of these things arose a perfectly truthful feeling of them as a whole, an intuitive knowledge of their solemn splendour and enervating melancholy.

The palm-tree was *recalled* to me, I believe for the first time, by an engraving in a child's book: *Les Jeunes Naturalistes* by Madame Ulliac-Trémadeure, one of my New Year's gifts out of which I loved to be read to in the evenings. Palms in hot-houses were as yet unknown in our little town. — The draughtsman had represented two of these unknown trees on a sea-shore, where some negroes were standing. Lately I had the curiosity to look again at this initiatory picture in the poor little book, its paper yellow with years and spotted with the damp of many winters; and I really wondered how it could have given rise to the very dimmest dream, unless my childish soul had been full of antecedent memories.

The colonies! How can I express everything that tried to struggle into being in my brain at the mere ring of the word. A fruit from the colonies, a bird, a shell, were to me forthwith objects almost of enchantment. There were quantities of these colonial treasures at Antoinette's home; a parrot, birds of all colours in a cage, collections of shells and insects. In her mother's drawers I had seen quaint strings of fragrant berries; and in the lofts where we would sometimes rummage together, we found the skins of beasts, queer bags, cases with the names of West Indian places still legible on them; and a vague exotic perfume pervaded the whole house. Her garden, as I have said was divided from ours by only a very low wall covered with roses and jasmine; and a pomegranate which grew there, a tall and venerable tree, threw its branches over our yard, and in the season shed its coral petals there.

We would often talk, behind the scenes, from one house to the other:

"May I go over and play with you, I say? Will your mamma let me?"

"No. I have been naughty, I am in disgrace...." This was very often the case. Then I felt greatly disappointed but less for her sake, I must own, than for the sake of the parrot and the foreign curiosities.

She herself had been born there — in the colonies, this very little Antoinette, and — how strange it seemed, — she did not appear to understand the value of the privilege; she was not delighted, she could scarcely remember anything about it. But I — I would have given anything in the world if only once, for a moment, my eyes might have had the briefest glimpse of those lands, so far away, so inaccessible as I felt they were. And with almost an anguish of regret — the regret of a marmoset in its cage — I would reflect that alas! in all my life as a minister, however long it might be, I should never see them, never.

XV.

I WILL tell you the game which most amused Antoinette and me during those two delicious summers.

It was this: first we were caterpillars; we crawled on the ground, with difficulty, on our hands and stomachs, searching for leaves to eat. Then we made believe that invincible sleepiness numbed our senses, and we lay down in some corner under the boughs, covering our heads with our white pinafores; we were chrysalises in our cocoons. This state lasted a longer or shorter time, and we so fully entered into our part of insects undergoing metamorphosis that a listener might have overheard such phrases as these spoken in tones of entire conviction:

"Do you think you will soon fly?"

"Oh, it will be very soon this time. I feel them on my shoulders—they are unfolding...."

They, of course, were wings.

At last we woke up; stretched ourselves with airs and graces, not speaking a word, but as if we were amazed at the phenomenon of this final transformation. And then, suddenly, we began to run about, hither and thither, very lightly in our little thin shoes; with our hands we held the corners of our white pinnies, fluttering them to "make believe" wings — and we ran and ran, flitting after each other or away again, across and across in sharp fantastic curves; close to every flower to smell it with the restless hurry of a butterfly, and making a buzzing noise, "Hooooo" with our lips nearly shut and our cheeks puffed out.

XVI.

BUTTERFLIES — poor butterflies, they are out of fashion now-a-days — played a very great part in my life as a child, I am ashamed to confess; with flies, beetles, dragon flies, all the creeping things of the grass and the flowers. Though I could not bear killing them I made collections of them, and I was always to be seen with a butterfly-net in my hand. Those which flitted into the back garden, excepting a stray specimen from the country now and then, were not, it must be owned, very handsome; but I had the garden and the woods of *la Limoise* which all the summer through were my happy hunting-grounds, full of surprises and marvels. However, Topffer's caricatures gave me pause; and when Lucette meeting me with a butterfly stuck into my hat would put on her inimitable mocking face and call me "Monsieur Cryptogame" I was deeply humiliated.

XVII.

THE poor old grandmamma who sang songs was dying.

We were standing round her bed, all of us, in the dusk of a spring day. She had not kept her bed more than eight-and-forty hours, but by reason of her great age the doctor said it meant a speedy end. Her brain had suddenly become quite clear; she mistook none of our names; she called us, bid us stay, in a gentle deliberate voice — her voice in the past, no doubt, which I had never known.

Standing by my father I gazed at my dying grandmother, and at the simple spacious room with its old-fashioned furniture. Above all I looked at the pictures on the walls, representing flowers in jars.

Oh! Those water-colours on my grandmother's walls, poor little innocent things! They all had this superscription: *"Bouquet à ma mère"* and below a few respectful lines of poetry dedicated to her — four lines, which I now could read and understand. These were works of my father's childhood and youth; for at every anniversary of her birthday he had contributed such a work to decorate their unpretending home. Poor little innocent things! They bore witness to the modest existence of those bygone days, and the sacred intimacy of the mother and son in the old time, on the morrow of their great trials, of the fearful wars, of English invaders and fire-ships. For the first time it now struck me that my grandmother might once have been young; that no doubt, before her brain had gone wrong, my father had loved her as I loved my mother; that his grief at losing her would be very great. I pitied him, and was sorry for having laughed at her songs, for having laughed at her talk to her looking-glass.

I was sent down stairs. On various pretexts I was kept out of the way all the evening without understanding why; then I was taken to our friends the D.'s, to dine with Lucette.

But when my nurse fetched me home, at about half-past eight, I would go straight up to my grandmother.

At the door I was at once struck by the perfect order which had been re-established, the atmosphere of profound peace which reigned in the room. In the shadows of the further side my father was sitting motionless by the head of the bed; the curtains hung straight and even, and on the pillow, just in the middle, I discerned my grandmother's face — asleep. Her attitude had something indescribable about it, too straight — final as it were, eternal.

Near the door my mother and sister were sewing at each side of a chiffonnier, in the place where they had sat ever since my grandmother had been taken ill. As I appeared they signed to me to be quiet: "Gently, gently; no noise; she is asleep." The lamp shade threw a bright light on their work which was a mass of scraps of silk — green, brown, yellow, grey — among which I recognized pieces of their old dresses, or their old bonnet-ribbons. At the first moment, I fancied these must be some objects which it was customary to prepare thus for dying persons; but as I questioned them in a whisper they explained: these were simply scent-bags they were preparing, and going to sew for a charitable ball.

I said that before going to bed I would go up to grandmother and try to bid her good-night, and they let me go a little way towards the bed;

but as I reached the middle of the room they suddenly thought better of it after exchanging glances:

"No, no," said they, still in a whisper, "Come away; you might disturb her."

But indeed, I had stopped of my own accord, startled and chilled — I had understood.

In spite of the horror which rooted me to the spot I was surprised that my grandmother was not unpleasant to look at; never having seen any one dead before I had always imagined that, the soul once departed, there must be from the first moment a haggard expressionless grimace like a death's-head. On the contrary, she had an infinitely sweet and happy smile; she was still pretty and looked young again — at perfect peace.

Then there passed through me one of those little lightning-flashes such as often gleam in a child's brain, as if to afford a furtive, questioning glance into uncertain depths; and I made this reflection: How could my grandmother be in Heaven? How was I to understand this division of the person, since what is left to be buried is so entirely herself, preserving, alas! even her expression?

So I stole away without asking any questions, my heart full and my soul distraught, not daring to hear the confirmation of what I had guessed so surely, and preferring not to hear the word which terrified me.

. . . .

For a long time little scent-bags were inseparable in my mind from the notion of death.

XVIII.

TO this day there lurk in my memory certain painful impressions, almost distressing if I concentrate my mind on them, of a serious illness I had when I was about eight years old. It was called scarlet-fever I was told, and the name alone struck me as having something diabolical about it.

It was in the bitter dismal season of March

squalls, and every evening at dusk, if my mother was by any chance not at my side, gloom fell on my soul. Oh! that twilight dejection which animals, and complicated creatures such as I, feel with almost equal intensity! My parted bed-curtains revealed in the foreground always the same depressing little table, with cups of *tisane*,* and phials of medicine. And as I lay gazing at this sick-room apparatus — growing more and more dim and vague and weird against the background of the darkening silent room — my head was filled with a procession of disconnected images, morbid and alarming. For two successive evenings I was visited in the half-light, in my feverish doze, by two different persons who filled me with terror.

First came an old lady humpbacked and very ugly, with an insinuating ugliness, who came up to me without a sound, without my hearing the door open or seeing the nurse who sat with me rise to receive her. She went away at once

---

* Cooling drinks prepared from violets, marshmallow, or other herbs.

without even speaking to me; but as she turned her back I saw her hump, and there was an opening at the top of it out of which perked the green head of a parrot the old lady had inside her, which said Cuckoo! in a little squeak like a speaking doll a long way off and then vanished again into that terrible back. — Oh! as I heard that Cuckoo! my forehead was damp with cold dews; but it was all gone, and I understood at once that it was but a dream.

The next night a man came, tall and lean, in a black gown like a priest. He did not come near; but he wandered round and round the room, quite close to the wall; very fast but making no sound, he was very much bent and his horrid legs, like sticks stuck his gown out stiffly as he hurried by. And — terror of terrors — his head was the great, white skull of a bird with a long bill — the monstrous and magnified image of a sea-mew's skull, bleached by the spray, which I had picked up the summer before on the beach of the island. — I believe this gentleman's visit coincided with the day when I was at the worst, even in some little danger. After a few rounds, always in the same hurry and the same silence, he rose from the floor still making play with his lean legs — higher, higher — on the cornice, the pictures, the mirrors — till he vanished in the ceiling, now quite dark.

Well, for two or three years the image of these two figures haunted me. In winter evenings I remembered them with alarm as I went up the stairs, which it was not yet usual to light up. "Supposing they should be there," I would say to myself; "supposing they were watching for me behind the doors so suspiciously ajar, either of them were to pursue me; supposing they should come up behind me, stretching out their hands from step to step to clutch my legs!"

And I declare I am not sure whether by the humouring of my fancy a little, I might not at this very day feel uneasy on those stairs about that old lady and gentleman, they were for so long the crowning features of my childish terrors, and so long headed the processions of my visions and bad dreams.

Many another gloomy apparition haunted the early years of my life, though it was so exceptionally happy. Many a sinister reverie would come upon me in the twilight; of a night with no morrow, of a short future with nothing beyond; thoughts of an early death. Too much petted and sheltered in a sort of intellectual hothouse, I displayed, as it were, an etiolated growth and the limp langour of a plant which lacks air. What I wanted was companions of my own age, rough, noisy little brutes of boys; instead of this I now and then played with only little girls, and was always prim and neat, my hair curled and my manners those of a little marquis of the XVIII century.

XIX.

AFTER this long fever, with its malignant name, I remember with rapture the day when at last I was allowed to breathe the outer air, to go down into my garden. It was now April, and they had chosen a brilliant day for my first outing, with a glorious sky. Under the trellices of jasmine and honeysuckle I felt the enchantment of Paradise, of Eden. Everything had sprouted and blossomed; without my knowing it, while I was shut up, the lovely *mise en scène* of revival had unfolded on the earth. This perennial phantasmagoria, which has soothed the soul of man for so many ages, and which only the very old ever cease to enjoy, had not yet very often beguiled me; and I gave myself up to it with perfect intoxication. Oh! that pure air, mild and balmy; that daylight, that sunshine; the lovely green of the young plants, the crowded leaves casting a new shade! And within me, reviving strength, and the joy of breathing, and the deep spring of life beginning once more.

My brother was at this time a tall fellow of twenty-one, who was free to do as he list. All the time I was ill I had been much excited over something he was doing in the garden and which I was dying to see. It was a miniature tank in a sweet nook under an old plum-tree; he had had it dug out and cemented like a reservoir; then he had had irregular stones brought in from the open heath, and turfs of moss, to build up a romantic edging of rock and grotto. And now it was all finished; gold fish were already swimming in it, and the little fountain was made to play for the first time in my honour.

I was quite enchanted; it was beyond every thing my imagination could have conceived of as most delightful. And when my brother told me that it was for me, that he gave it me for my own, I felt a depth of joy which it seemed to me must last for ever. To possess all this! What unlooked-for happiness! To rejoice in it every day, day after day, during the fine hot months that were coming. And to live out of doors again, to play as I had done last summer in every corner of the place thus beautified.

I stayed a long time by the side of my pond, never tired of looking, admiring, breathing the soft spring air; elated with the broad daylight I had forgotten and the sunshine I had found again; while over my head the old tree, planted long ago by some ancestor and already somewhat dry, spread its pierced screen of young leaves against the blue sky, and the tiny fountain went on with its purling tinkle in the shade like a little hurdy-gurdy singing with glee at my return to life.

Now-a-days the poor plum-tree, after languishing with old age is quite dead, and the stump, which is all that is left standing, cherished out of respect, is crowned like a ruin with a clump of ivy. But the pond with its banks and islets remains untouched; time has only given it an appearance of genuineness. The moss-grown stones pretend to be very ancient indeed; real water weeds, the tender growths of springs, have made themselves at home there, with rushes and wild iris; and dragon-flies that have wandered into the town take refuge there. It is a tiny plot of uncultured nature which has established itself there, and which is never disturbed.

And to me it is the spot of earth to which I am most fondly attached, after having loved many others; there I am at peace as I am nowhere else; there I find refreshment, the renewal of youth and of life. My Mecca, my holy place, is that little plot; so much so that if it were altered I feel that something in my life would have lost its balance, I should miss my foothold — it would be the beginning of the end.

The absolute consecration of the place arose, I fancy, from my seafaring life; my long voyages, and frequent exiles during which I always thought of it and pictured it with affection.

To one of these miniature grottoes I especially cling with peculiar devotion. I so often dreamed of it in hours of dejection and melancholy in the course of my wanderings. After the breath of Azrael had so cruelly passed over us, after misfortunes of every kind, after so many years during which I tossed about the world while my widowed mother and my aunt Claire, two black figures, were left alone in the dear old house, now almost empty and as still as the tomb — in those long years, more than once I had felt a chill about my heart as I thought that the deserted hearth and all the places dear to my childhood were no doubt falling into neglected decay; but above all I longed to know whether the hand of time and the winter rains had destroyed the slight roof of that little grotto. It is a strange thing to say, but if those mimic rocks, old and moss-grown, had fallen in, I should have felt almost as if an irremediable fissure had been made in my life.

By the side of the little pool an old grey wall forms part of what I have called my Mecca; it is, I might almost say, the very heart of it. I know its minutest details; the microscopic lichens which grow there, and the rifts made by time where spiders are at home; for an arbour of ivy and honeysuckle grows up against it in whose shade I was wont to settle myself to my tasks in the finest summer days, and then, during my idling as a not very studious school-boy, its grey stones absorbed my whole attention with their infinitely little world of insects and mosses. Not only do I love and venerate this old wall, as the Arabs do their holiest mosque, but I fancy it protects me, secures my life, and prolongs my youth. I would not suffer the smallest change to be made in it, and if it were taken down I should feel it as the destruction of a mainstay which nothing could ever replace. This is no doubt because the mere continuance of certain things which we have known all our lives, beguiles us at last as to our own permanence, our own continuance; seeing them unchanged, we fancy that we cannot change either, nor cease to be. I find no other explanation of this feeling which is almost fetichism.

And yet, good Heavens! when I reflect — these stones are, after all, any stones; brought together like those of any wall, by workmen, no matter who, a century perhaps before I was born — then I feel how childish is the illusion I indulge in spite of myself, that they have any protecting charm; on how instable a foundation — an airy nothing — I dream that my life depends.

Men who have never had a paternal home, who, while still young, have gone from place to place and lived under hired roofs, can obviously understand nothing of these feelings. But among those who have preserved the family hearth there must, I am sure, be many who, without owning it to themselves, are conscious of similar impressions in various degrees. Like me they store up their own evanescence on the relative antiquity of an old garden wall loved in childhood, an old terrace they have always known, an old tree unchanged in growth.

And to others alas! before them, the same things perhaps had afforded their illusory probation, to unknown predecessors, now mingling with the dust, and who were not even of their blood or of their race.

XX.

IT was after this illness, about the middle of that summer, that I paid my longest visit to the *island*. I was sent thither with my brother, and with my sister who was like a second mother to me. After spending a few days with our relations at Saint-Pierre d'Oleron — my grand-aunt Claire and the two old maids her daughters — we three went to live together on the *Grand'-Côte* — the ocean coast — in a fishing village, then perfectly unknown and remote from outer ken.

The *Grand'-Côte* or *Côte-Sauvage* is the side of the island which overlooks the infinite ocean horizon; which is perennially swept by the westerly gale. The strand stretches without a curve, straight and endless, and the breakers come in unchecked till they reach the shore, as majestic as on the coast of Sahara, and curl over in melancholy mile-long rollers of white surf, with a loud unceasing noise. A stern region with desert spaces; a region of sand where stunted trees, dwarf evergreen oaks, cower under shelter of the sand-hills. A quite peculiar flora, and all through the summer a profusion of fragrant little pinks. Only two or three villages with the wilderness between; hamlets of low houses, as white with lime-wash as the Algerian kasbahs, and surrounded by plots of such flowers as can withstand the salt breeze. They are inhabited by tanned fisher-folk, a brave and honest raçe, and still very primitive at the time of which I write, for no bathers had ever invaded these shores.

In an old, forgotten note-book in which my sister had written her impressions of that summer — they might have been my own — I find this description of our lodgings:

We were in the middle of the village at the house of Monsieur the Mayor. For Monsieur the Mayor's house had two wings of considerable extent.

It blazed in the sunshine, quite dazzling with lime-wash; its ponderous shutters, fastened with strong iron hooks, were painted dark green, after the fashion of the island. A garden plot was enclosed, like a garland round the house, and the flowers throve bravely in the sand: Marvel of Peru, its pretty branches of yellow, pink or crimson flowers rising from a tangle of mignonette, opened at noon with a faint scent of orange blossom.

Opposite, a little sandy cut went steeply down to the strand.

It is from this stay on the open coast that I date my first really intimate acquaintance with wrack, and crabs, and sea anemonies, and all the thousand treasures of the shore.

That summer, too, I first fell in love — with a little girl in the village. But here again, that the tale may be more true, I will allow my sister to speak, and copy from the old note-book:

The fisher folks' children would come out in dozens, brown and tanned, trotting along with their little bare feet, following Pierre, or boldly getting in front of him and looking back from time to time, opening their fine black eyes very wide. In those days *a little gentleman* was a sight so rare in that part of the world as to be well worth running after.

Down the sandy hollow-way Pierre went to shore every morning, surrounded by this escort. He would rush on the shells, which are exquisite on this tract of sand; yellow, pink and violet — of every fresh and delicate hue and the most delicate shapes. He would find some that were a perfect delight to him, and the little ones in utter silence would fill their hands with them, too, and follow him, never saying a word.

One of the most constant was Véronique — about his own age, perhaps a little younger, six or seven. She had a sweet, dreamy little face, dark and pale, with lively grey eyes; all hooded in a deep white *kichenote* — an old local name for a sun bonnet, an ancient head-dress of the women of the coast. Véronique would creep close up to Pierre and at last take possession of his hand, and would not leave go again. They trotted on as two babies do which have taken a fancy for each other, saying nothing, but looking at each other from time to time — then a kiss now and then. *Voudris ben vous biser* — I should like to kiss you, she would say, putting out her little arms with touching affection; and Pierre let her give him a kiss, and returned it warmly on her nice, round little cheeks.

Véronique ran off to sit down on our door step every morning as soon as she was up; she huddled down like a little dog and waited. Pierre, as soon as he woke felt sure she was there, and for her he would be up quite early; he must be washed and his yellow hair combed — quick, very quick, and off he went to find his little friend. They hugged and then talked over all they had found the day before; sometimes Véronique, before coming to her seat, had already been down to the shore and gathered fresh treasures hidden in her pinafore.

One day, towards the end of August, after long musing, weighing, no doubt, and settling all the difficulties which might arise from differences of social status, Pierre said: "Véronique, we will be married; I will ask leave of Papa and Mamma."

My sister goes on to give this account of our departure:

On the 15th of September we had to leave. Pierre had made piles of shells, seaweeds, starfish, pebbles; insatiable, he wanted to bring everything away, and packed it all into boxes; he and Véronique, who helped him with all her might.

One morning a large carriage came from Saint-Pierre to fetch us away, rousing the peaceful village by the tinkling of bells and the smacking of the whip. Pierre anxiously saw all his personal belongings stowed in it, and we all three got in; his eyes already full of grief looked down the hollow cut to the sands — and at his little friend who was sobbing.

And to end I will transcribe, again word for word, this reflection of my sister's, written in that same summer, at the end of the note-book, and faded by years:

Then there came over me — and not for the first time — an uneasy wondering as I looked at Pierre. I asked myself: "What will that child be? — And what his little friend, whose outline is to be seen still standing at the end of the road? What despair is racking that tiny heart; what anguish at finding herself thus deserted."

"What will that child be?" Good God! nothing but just what he was at that very day; in the after years nothing more, and nothing less. Departures like that one; busy packing of a thousand treasures of no appreciable value; the craving to carry everything away, to bear about a whole world of souvenirs—and above all adieux to those little untamed creatures, loved just because they were so—: this is the epitome of my whole life.

The two or three days of our return journey, including a pause to see our old island aunts, seemed to me infinitely long. My impatience to see my mother once more deprived me of sleep. More than two months without seeing her! My sister in those days was the only person in the world who could have enabled me to endure so long a separation.

When we were on the mainland once more, after three hours drive from the shore where a boat deposited us, when the carriage conveying us had passed the ramparts of the town — at last I saw my mother waiting for us, her eyes, her sweet smile. — And in the distant past one of the dearest indelible images I can always recall is her dear face, still almost young, and her dear hair still black.

As soon as I got home I ran to see my little lake and grottoes, and the arbour behind, against the old wall. But my eyes had slowly become accustomed to the immense stretches of seashore; everything looked shrunk, diminished, shut in, melancholy. And the leaves were turning yellow; there was an indefinable touch of early autumn in the air, and yet very hot. I thought with dread of the dark cold days to come, and very sadly set to work in the court-yard to unpack my boxes of sea-weeds or shells, full of stricken regret at no longer being in the island. I was uneasy, too, about Véronique, and what she would do all alone during the winter; suddenly I was moved to tears at the remembrance of her poor little sunburnt hand which would never again rest in mine.

XXI.

THE beginning of tasks, lessons, copy-books, ink-spots — what a sudden dreariness in my story. Of all that I have none but sullen recollections, mortally wearisome. And if I dared to be quite sincere, I might say the same I believe of my teachers themselves. Oh! Heavens! The first who taught me Latin — *rosa*, a rose, *cornu*, the horn, *tonitru*, the thunder — a tall old man, bent, unwashed, and dismal to behold as rain in November! He is dead, poor fellow, peace be to his soul; he was a realization of Töpffer's " Monsieur Ratin" — in every detail, to the wart with three hairs at the end of his old nose which displayed an inconceivable complication of wrinkles. He was to me the personification of all that was disgusting and repulsive.

Every day he came precisely at noon; his pull of the bell chilled my blood; I should have known it among a thousand. After his departure

I myself purified that part of my table where his elbows had rested, wiping it with napkins which I clandestinely carried off to the dirty linen room. And this aversion extended even to the books — in themselves not attractive — which he had touched; I tore out some pages which I suspected of having been too long in contact with his hands.

My books were always full of blots, always soiled, untidy, covered with scrawls and scribbling such as the pen will execute when the mind is wandering. I, such a neat and careful child in all else, had such a contempt for these books I was condemned to read that, with regard to them, I was vulgar and ill-behaved. And moreover — which is stranger still, my conscience was nowhere with regard to my tasks; they were always done at the last moment, anyhow; my aversion for study was the first thing which tempted me to compromise my scruples.

However, everything went on well, more or less; my lessons, at which I glanced at the last extremity, were pretty well learnt. And as a rule

"Monsieur Ratin" wrote *good* or *pretty good* on the mark-book which I had to show to my father every evening.

But I really believe that if he, or the other tutors who came after him, could have suspected the truth, could have imagined that, once out of their sight, my mind never dwelt for five minutes in the day perhaps on the things they taught me, the indignation of their honest souls must have found utterance.

XXII.

IN the course of the winter after my return from the coast of the island a great event took place in our family life, the departure of my brother for his first campaign.

He was, as I have said, my elder by about fourteen years. Perhaps I had not had time enough to know him well, to become really attached to him, for he began to lead the life of a young man very early, and this separated us. I never went into his room, where the number of big books spread about the table and the smell of his cigars appalled me, and I ran the risk of meeting his companions, officers or students. I heard, too, that he was not always good, that he sometimes stayed out late at night, and had in consequence to be lectured, and secretly I disapproved of his conduct.

But his approaching departure increased my affection for him, and I was really sorry.

He was going to Polynesia, to Tahiti, to the very end of the world, the opposite side of the globe, and he was to be away for four years, which represented about half my life and seemed to me almost an indefinite absence.

I took a particular interest in the preparations for this long campaign: the iron-bound cases which were packed with such care; the gold braid and embroideries, his sword, which was shrouded with tissue paper and buried like a mummy in a tin case, all this increased the impressions I had formed of the danger and distance of his long voyage.

Moreover, a weight of melancholy hung over

the whole household and became heavier and heavier as the day of separation approached. Our meals were eaten in silence, excepting now and then a piece of advice was given, and I listened thoughtfully and said nothing.

The evening before he left, he amused himself, and greatly honored me — by confiding to my care various little fragile knick-knacks on his mantel-piece, begging me to see they were not damaged in his absence.

Then he made me a present of a large book with a gilt cover which was called *Travels in Polynesia*, full of pictures; and this was the only book I loved as a little child. I turned over the pages at once with eager curiosity. At the beginning, a large picture represented a rather pretty woman, with brown complexion, crowned with grasses and lounging under a palm-tree, and underneath was written: "Portrait of H. M. Pomaré IV, Queen of Tahiti." Further on were two beautiful creatures on the seashore, with bare bosoms and heads crowned with flowers, with the inscription: "Tahitian girls on the beach."

The last hour on the day he left, the preparations being finished and the big boxes locked, we assembled in the drawing-room in solemn silence. A chapter of the Bible was read and then family prayers . . . Four years! and soon the width of the world between us and him.

I remember particularly my mother's face during this farewell scene; seated in an arm-chair with him beside her, she kept at first after prayers an infinitely sad smile, an expression of resigned confidence, but suddenly a change I had not expected came over her features and she burst into tears. I had never before seen her cry and was terribly distressed.

The first days which followed I was oppressed with the void he had left; from time to time I looked into his empty room, and as for the different little things he had either given or confided to me, they became most sacred relics.

I was shown on a map of the world his passage which would take about five months. As for his return, I only saw it in an unimaginable and unreal future; and, strangely enough, what most spoiled the prospect of his return, was the fact that I should be twelve or thirteen years old, quite a big boy when I saw him again.

Unlike all other children, especially those of the present day — who are in such a hurry to become little men and women — I had even then that horror of growing up, which became more marked later on; I used even to talk and write about it, but when asked why, I could only reply, not knowing better how to explain it: "I think I shall be so bored when I am grown up!" I believe it is a very singular case, unique perhaps, this dread of life, from its commencement: I could not clearly see the horizon, I could not give any shape, however vague, to the future; before me everything was impenetrably black, a leaden curtain was spread over the darkness.

XXIII.

"CAKES, cakes, beautiful cakes, all hot!"
Thus sang to a plaintive air composed by herself, the old woman who sold them, and who

for the first ten or fifteen years of my life, passed regularly under our windows on winter evenings.

Whenever I think of those evenings, that melancholy little ditty sung behind the scenes, rushes into my mind.

It is more particularly in connection with Sundays that the song of *cakes all hot* presents itself; for those evenings, having no tasks to do, I spent with my parents in the drawing-room on the ground-floor, which looked into the street, so when, at nine o'clock, the little old woman passed by, her sonorous chant echoing in the silent frosty night, I was there close enough to hear.

She foretold the cold in the same way that the swallows announce the spring; after the chill autumn, the first time we heard her song, we said: "Now winter has come."

In those evenings, the drawing-room, as I knew it then, was large, and to me appeared immense. Very simple, but arranged with a good deal of taste: the walls and woodwork colored brown with a dull gold beading, furniture upholstered in red velvet, which must have dated from the time of Louis-Philippe; the family portraits in stiff black and gold frames. Severe bronze ornaments on the chimney-piece; and on the middle table, in the place of honour, a large XVIth century Bible, a venerable relic of the Huguenot ancestors who were persecuted for the faith; and flowers, always baskets and vases of flowers at a time when these things were not yet the fashion as they are now.

After dinner, it was a delicious moment when we came in there out of the dining-room; everything had such a comfortable peaceful air; and when all the family were seated, grandmother and aunts in a circle, I began gamboling in the middle on the red carpet for mere joy at being in the midst of them, and in longing impatiently for the little games that would be played for my sake in a few minutes. Our neighbors the D***s, passed every Sunday evening with us; it was a family tradition, one of those time-honoured provincial friendships which have existed for generations and are handed down with the heirlooms.

Towards eight o'clock, when I heard their well-known ring, I jumped for joy, and nothing could have prevented my rushing to the front door to receive them, and in particular my great friend Lucette, who, of course, came with her parents.

Alas! how sadly I now review those loved or venerated forms, God bless them! — who used to surround me on Sunday evenings; most of them have disappeared, and their faces, that I would fain remember, fade in spite of me, become hazy and disappear too. . . .

Well, we began the games, to please me, the only child present; we played at *marriage, my lady's toilet, the horned lady, the beautiful shepherdess, blind-man's buff*, everybody taking part, even the most elderly; Grand-aunt Bertha, the oldest member and quite the funniest.

And all of a sudden I stopped short, listening attentively as in the distance I heard: — *Cakes, cakes, beautiful cakes, all hot!*

It came closer and closer, for the singer ran, steadily but quickly; quite soon she was under our windows, repeating the same song in her high cracked voice.

And it was one of my great amusements, not to get some one to buy me some of those poor cakes — for they were rather heavy and I did not much care for them — but to run myself, when I was allowed, to the front door, accompanied by a willing aunt to stop the cake woman.

With a curtsey she would come up, good old soul, proud at being called, and put her basket down on the steps; her clean costume was finished off with white linen over-sleeves. Then, while she uncovered her wares, I, like a caged bird, cast a longing look outside into the cold deserted street. There was the whole charm; a breath of freezing air, a glance into the black darkness, and then to rush back into the warm and comfortable drawing-room — while the monotonous refrain grew fainter and fainter and then died away, every evening in the same direction, through the same squalid streets, in the neighbourhood of the port and the ramparts. Her road was always the same, — and my thoughts followed her with a singular interest as long as her song, which she repeated from minute to minute, could be heard at all.

This attention was mingled with pity for the poor old woman who took this nightly walk,—but there was another sentiment mixed with it,—oh! so confused and vague that I may seem to give it too much importance, even in slightly sketching it. I had a queer curiosity to know more about those low quarters of the town, to which the cake-seller went so bravely, and where I was never taken. Old streets seen from a distance, deserted by day, but where from time immemorial the sailors had a riotous time on fête-day evenings, the noise of their songs sometimes reaching us. What went on there? What were the brutal games of which we heard the cries? What did they play at, those folks returned from sea, or from far tropical lands? What a rough, simple and free life was theirs?—To put all this in the right focus, you must dilute it, or wrap it, so to speak, in a white veil. Already I felt the germ of a trouble, an aspiration towards an unknown something, and on returning to the drawing-room, where they sat quietly talking, for an instant, hardly appreciable, it seemed to me, I was a prisoner in a hot-house.

At half-past nine, rarely later on my account, tea was brought in, with thin slices of bread and butter, — such delicious butter, and cut with a nicety that there is never time to give to anything in these days. Then about eleven, after a chapter from the Bible and prayers, we went to bed.

In my little white bed, I was more fidgety on Sunday evenings than any other. First there was the prospect of M. Ratin's return, more painful to contemplate after the respite; then I regretted that this day of rest was already over, so quickly past, and I hated to think of the lessons to be done every day for a whole week before Sunday could come again. Sometimes, too, in the distance, some sailors would pass singing, and thus change the current of my ideas; and I thought of the colonies, and ships, and I had a sort of dim inexplicable longing — latent, if I may use the word — to rush in search of adventure and amusement, out into the keen night air of winter, or into the blazing sunshine of tropical ports; and sing, at the top of my voice as they did, the simple joy of being alive.

XXIV.

"*AND I beheld, and heard an angel flying through the midst of heaven, saying with a loud voice, Woe, woe, woe, to the inhabiters of the earth!*"

Besides the reading in the family circle every evening, I read a chapter of the Bible every morning in bed.

My Bible was a little one with small print. Between the pages I had pressed some treasured dried flowers; one particular branch of beautiful pink larkspur had the gift of clearly bringing to my recollection the stubblefield* on the isle of Oleron, where I had gathered it.

The "stubble" of the island, inhabited by

* Gleux.

swarms of grasshoppers, is covered with a late crop of tall blue cornflowers, and above all, of larkspurs, white, violet or pink.

So on winter mornings in bed, before beginning my reading I always looked at this branch of flowers, whose colour was hardly faded, and it brought back to me the fields of Oleron and the blazing summer sunshine. . .

"*And I beheld, and heard an angel flying through the midst of heaven, saying with a loud voice, Woe, woe, woe, to the inhabiters of the earth!*"

"*And the fifth angel sounded, and I saw a star fall from heaven unto the earth; and to him was given the key of the bottomless pit.*"

When I read my Bible alone and could choose the passage, I always selected the grand account in Genesis of the creation of light from darkness, or else the marvellous visions in the Apocalypse; I was fascinated by the poetry of these dreams of terror, which have no equal, to my knowledge, in any human book — the beast with seven heads, the signs in heaven, the sound of the last trumpet, these terrors I knew so well, haunted and charmed my imagination. — There was a book of the last century, a relic of my Huguenot ancestors in which I saw these things depicted: a *History of the Bible* with quaint apocalyptic pictures where all in the distance was black. My maternal grandmother treasured, in a cupboard in her room, this precious volume which she had brought from the isle, and as I was in the habit of repairing thither in a melancholy mood in the winter when it began to be dusk, it was nearly always when the light was failing that I asked her lend it me, and on her knees, until it was too dark to see, I turned the yellow pages and looked at the flights of angels with their large strong wings, the black curtains, foreboding the end of the world, the sky darker than the earth, and in the midst of the banks of clouds, the simple and terrible triangle signifying Jehovah.

XXV.

EGYPT, Ancient Egypt especially, a little later on, exercised a weird fascination over me, I recognized it for the first time, without astonishment or hesitation in an engraving in an illustrated magazine. I greeted as old acquaintances, two gods with hawks-heads whom I met there, depicted in profile on a stone, one on each side of a strange zodiac, and though the day was dark, they brought I am sure, an immediate impression of heat and sunshine.

XXVI.

AFTER my brother was gone, during the following winter, I spent many of my play-hours in his room, painting the prints in the book of Voyages in Polynesia which he had given me.

First I coloured the flowers and the birds with extreme care. Then it was the turn of the men. As to the "Young Girls of Tahiti on the seashore," which the designer had drawn from some imaginary nymphs, I made them white — oh as white and pink as the sweetest dolls. And I thought them quite bewitching. The future had it in store to show me that they were of a different hue, and that their charm is of another kind.

But, indeed, all my notions of beauty have changed greatly since then, and I should have been much amazed if I had been told what kinds of faces I should have come to think charming in the unforeseen sequel. All children have the same ideal on that point, which varies as they grow to be men. They, in their simplicity and purity, look only for regular features and fresh, rosy complexions; later their tastes are various, according to their culture of mind, and still more, the impulses of their senses.

XXVII.

I NO longer remember exactly at what date I founded my Museum, which for a long time was my chief amusement. Rather higher up than my Aunt Bertha's room was a little attic quite apart, of which I took entire possession; the charm of the room lay in its window, which looked out, high up, to the west, over the old trees on the ramparts, and the remoter meadows where russet specks scattered on the level green, indicated oxen and cows, wandering herds. I had persuaded my parents to have this attic prepared for me, with a pinkish fawn-colored paper which remains to this day, and to have shelves and glass cases fixed. Here I placed my butterflies which I thought very precious specimens; I set up birds' nests found in the woods of *la Limoise;* shells picked up on the shores of the island, and others brought home long before by unknown relations, and disinterred in the loft from the depths of ancient sea-chests where they had been slumbering for years in the dust. In this little domain I spent many hours, alone, and quiet, lost in contemplation of exotic mother-of-pearl shells, dreaming of the lands whence they had come, and picturing to myself those strange shores.

A kind old grand-uncle, only a distant relation but very fond of me, encouraged me in these amusements. He was a doctor, and having lived for a long time in his youth on the coast of Africa, he himself had a collection of Natural History far more interesting than many a town museum. Wonderful things were there: rare shells and curious amulets, weapons still reeking of the strange smells with which I have since been saturated; matchless butterflies in glass frames.

He lived but a little way off and I often went to see him. To get to his museum we had to cross his garden where daturas and opuntias flourished, and where a grey parrot from the Gaboon lived, talking in a negro lingo.

And when the old man told me about Senegal, and Gorea, and Guinea, the music of these names went to my head, a foretaste of the heavy gloom of the dark continent. He, my poor old uncle, predicted that I should become a learned naturalist — and he was greatly mistaken, as so many others have been who prophesied my future. He, indeed, was further from the mark than any one; he did not understand that my love of natural history was merely a temporary digression of my fluctuating little fancies; that glass cases, and dry classification, and dead science, had nothing in them that could attach me for long! — No, what attracted me was something behind these rigid objects — behind and beyond them; it was Nature herself, terrible and many-faced, the unknown immensity of forests and animal life.

XXVIII.

AT the same time I spent long hours, alas! ostensibly in doing my lessons.

Töpffer, the only school-boy's poet, so generally misunderstood, divides them into three classes: First, those at school. Secondly, those who work at home in a room, looking out on some dismal court-yard with perhaps a hoary old fig-tree. Thirdly, those who work at home, but whose bright little room looks out on the street.

I was in this last category, which Töpffer speaks of as a privileged class, likely to fill the world with the most cheerful men. My room, as a child, was on the first floor facing the street; white curtains, a green paper with bunches of white roses; near my window my writing-table and above this my much neglected book-shelf. As long as the weather was fine this window was always open and the shutters half-shut to allow of my constantly looking out without my idleness being remarked upon or reported by some unmannerly neighbor. So from morning till evening I could gaze on the quiet street basking in the sun between the white houses of a country town, and ending at the trees on the ramparts; at the rare passers-by, all known to me by sight; the various cats of the neighbourhood prowling about the doorsteps or on the roofs, the swifts wheeling in the hot air, and the swallows skimming over the dusty pavement. How many hours have I spent at that window, my mind absent in the vague day-dreams of an imprisoned sparrow, while my blotted copybook lay open with the first words only of an exercise which would not get done, of a composition which would not flow.

Then, of course, came a period of practical jokes on the passers-by; the inevitable result of my dull idleness — not unchequered by remorse. But I must confess that my great friend, Lucette, was very ready to take her share in these practical jokes. Though a young lady now of sixteen or seventeen she was sometimes still as great a babe as I was. "But mind you never tell!" she would impress upon me with an indescribably mischievous wink of her roguish eyes — I may tell now, when years have gone by and the flowers of twenty summers have withered on her tomb.

We began by making up neat little parcels, carefully wrapped in clean paper, and firmly tied with pink ribbon; inside were cherry-stalks, plum-stones, any such little rubbish; then we dropped them out of window and hid behind the shutters to see who would pick them up.

After this we wrote letters absolutely incoherent and nonsensical, with illustrations in the text, and which we slyly deposited on the pavement, addressed to the different oddities who lived near, at the hour when they were in the habit of passing by.

Oh! the mad laugh we used to have as we composed these effusions!—But, indeed, I have never met any one since Lucette with whom I could laugh so heartily—and almost always over things of which the hardly perceptible fun would not have brought a smile to any one else. Besides our faithful alliance of small brother and elder sister, we had in common a turn for light humour, a perfectly sympathetic sense of the incoherent and ridiculous. To me she had more wit than any one, and a single word would set us off laughing at a neighbour's expense, or at our own, in sudden joyous mirth till we could no more and dropped with exhaustion.

All this I admit was not in keeping with gloomy apocalyptic reveries and religious controversies. But even then I was a creature of inconsistencies.

Poor little Lucette or Luçon — Luçon was a noun proper, masculine, singular, which I had devised to call her by: 'My dear fellow, Luçon,' I used to say. — Poor little Lucette, she, too, was one of my teachers, but one of whom I felt neither disgust nor alarm. She, like M. Ratin, had a note-book in which she wrote *good* or *very good*, and which I had to show my parents every evening. For I forgot to mention sooner that she had amused herself by teaching me to play the piano when I was still quite tiny, in secret that I might, for a surprise on the occasion of some family festival, play the tunes of *Le Petit Suise* and *Le Rocher de Saint-Malo*. As a result she had been requested to continue the work she had begun so well, and my musical education was carried on by her till the time when I began to play Chopin and Liszt.

Painting and music were the only branches of

learning at which I really worked a little. My sister taught me to paint; but I do not remember its beginnings, I was so very young. I feel as though I had all my life been able to express on paper with pencil and paint-brush the fancies of my imagination.

XXIX.

IN my grandmother's room, at the back of the cupboard full of treasures where that terrible book of the Apocalypse was kept — the *Bible History* — there were other very venerable possessions. In the first place there was an ancient copy of the Psalms, a tiny volume with silver clasps, like a doll's book, which must have been a marvel of typography in its day. It was made so small, I was told, to be hidden with the greater ease; at the time of the persecutions ancestors of ours had often carried it about with them, concealed in their dress. Then, and above all, there were in a cardboard box a bundle of letters written on parchment, stamped Leyden or Amsterdam, and dating from 1702-10, with large wax seals bearing a monogram with a count's coronet. Letters, these, of Huguenot forefathers, who at the revocation of the edict of Nantes, had left their lands, their friends, their country — everything in the world, to adhere to their faith. They had written them to an old grandfather, too aged to tread the path of exile, and who had, I know not how, been able to remain in peace in the island of Oleron. They were submissive and reverential to him as no one dreams of being in these days, asking his advice and consent on every point — even his permission to wear a particular fashion of wigs which had come up in Amsterdam just then. Then they related all their concerns, with never a murmur, with evangelical resignation; their property being confiscated, they were obliged to embark in trade to make a living, and they hoped, they said, by God's blessing, to have enough for their children to live on.

Besides the respect I felt for these letters, they had for me the charm of very old things; it seemed to me so strange thus to penetrate to the root of that old-world existence, that inmost home-life, now a century and a half old.

And then, as I read, indignation filled my heart against the Roman Church, against Papal Rome, the Sovereign Power of the past, so clearly designated — at any rate to my apprehension — by the amazing apocalyptic description — "And the beast is a city, and its seven heads are the seven mountains on which the woman sitteth."

Grandmother herself, always so austere and erect, in her black gown, exactly as we always picture old Huguenot dames, had had some fears for her creed at the time of the restoration; and though she, too, never complained, it was certain that she had distressful memories of that time.

Moreover, in the island, I had been shown under the shade of a clump of trees enclosed by walls, and close to our old family home, a spot where many of my ancestors lay sleeping, having been excluded from the Church cemeteries for having died in the Protestant faith.

How, owning such a past, could I be otherwise than stanch? And it is very certain that if the Inquisition had been revived I should have endured martyrdom like a little visionary. My faith, indeed, was that of a pioneer; I was far from sharing my ancestors' resignation; in spite of my general aversion for reading I was often found deep in works of religious controversy; I knew by heart many passages of the Fathers, and the decisions of the early Councils of the Church. I could have discussed dogmas like a theologian, and was versed in arguments against the Papacy.

And yet a chill was beginning to fall on me; at church, especially, a grey blank seemed to enfold me. The tedium of certain Sunday sermons; the soullessness of the prayers prepared beforehand and uttered with conventional unction and appropriate gesticulation; the indifference of the people in their Sunday clothes who came to listen — how soon — and with what deep pain, what cruel disappointment — I felt the sickening formalism of it all. The very aspect of the church depressed me. A town church — a *temple* as the Protestant places of worship are called in France — quite new, with an attempt at being ornate, but not daring to be too decorative; I remember particularly certain mural ornaments which I positively loathed, which I shuddered to behold. It was the precursor of the feelings with which, only aggravated to excess, I at a later day sat in the Protestant churches of Paris and noted their attempt at elegance — and the beadles at the door with shoulder-knots! Oh! for the meetings in the Cévennes! Oh! for the *pastors of the Desert!*

Such trifles as these, of course, could not shake my convictions, which seemed to be as firmly founded as a house on a rock; but they gave rise to the first imperceptible rift through which, drop by drop, an icy damp began to ooze.

The place where I still could find true devoutness, the real and restful peace of the House of God, was the old Protestant church of Saint-Pierre d'Oleron; my grandfather Samuel, in the days of the persecution, must often have worshipped there, and my mother had attended the services all through her early life. — I also liked those little village chapels to which we sometimes went on Sundays in the summer; most of them very old, with bare, white, lime-washed walls; built no matter where — at the edge of a cornfield, wild flowers growing all round them, or hidden away at the bottom of a garden, at the end of an avenue of ancestral trees. The Catholics themselves have nothing which can excel in charm the humble sanctuaries of our Protestant sea-board — not even those most exquisite chapels of granite buried in the woods of Brittany, which I admired so much at a later date.

I was still quite determined to be a minister; in the first place I thought it my duty. I had promised and vowed it in my prayers; could I break my word? But when my little brain tried to plan the future, which seemed more and more wrapped in impenetrable darkness, my fancy always dwelt in preference on a home somewhat apart from the world, where the faith of my flock should still be simple, and my humble church hallowed by a long past of prayer.

In the island of Oleron for instance—

Yes, there, in the island of Oleron, in the midst of the memorials of my Huguenot forefathers, there I could look forward with greater ease and less dread to a life sacrificed to the service of the Lord.

XXX.

MY brother had reached the Delightful Island. His first letter from beyond seas, a very long one, on very thin paper, and yellow with the voyage, had been four months on its way to us.

It was an event in our family life; I can remember now, how, while my father and mother were opening it below, I joyfully flew upstairs to call grandmother and aunts down from their rooms.

Inside the envelope, so full of sheets and covered all over with American stamps, there was a little note for me, and on opening it I found a dried flower, a five-petaled star, faded and pale, but still pink. This flower, my brother told me, had grown and bloomed close to his window, actually inside his Tahitian cabin into which the lovely greenery of that zone forced its way. Oh, with what strange eagerness — with what curiosity as I may say, did I gaze at and touch this periwinkle which came as a fragment still vivid, still almost living of that remote and unknown Nature! — Then I put it away, with so much care that I have it to this day.

And when, after many years, I made a pilgrimage to the hut which my brother had lived in on the other side of the world I found, in fact, that the shady plot which surrounded it was pink with such periwinkles, that they crept over the threshold and blossomed within the deserted home.

XXXI.

WHEN my ninth year was complete there was for a short time some talk of sending me to school, to break me in to the miseries of the world; and while this was in the air I lived for a few days in terror of that prison, knowing the outside of it by its walls and the windows closed by iron bars. But on due reflection, it was decided that I was too delicate and precious a blossom to be exposed to contact with other children, who might have rough games and rude manners; so it was settled that I was still to stay at home.

However, I was delivered from M. Ratin. A good old tutor, with a round face, took his place; he displeased me less, but I did not work any the more. In the afternoon, when the hour of his coming was near, after scrambling through my exercises I would post myself at my window to watch for him from behind my shutters, with my lesson-book open at the piece I had to learn; and as soon as I spied him in the offing — round a corner at the furthest end of the street — I began to study it. And generally by the time he came in I knew it well enough to have a "pretty good" mark, which saved me from a scolding.

I also had an English master who came every morning, and whom I called Aristogiton — why, I never knew. Teaching me on the Robertsonian method, he made me paraphrase the History of Sultan Mahmoud. He, indeed, was the one person who thoroughly understood the situation; he was entirely convinced that I was doing nothing, less than nothing. But he had the good taste to make no complaints, and my gratitude soon became real affection.

In the summer, when the days were very hot, it was in the garden that I made believe to work; I loaded a certain green table under an arbour of ivy vine and honeysuckle, with copy-books, and blotted and ink-stained volumes. And as I was admirably situated for idling in perfect safety — all danger could be discerned so far off through the trellice and green branches, while I could not be seen — I took care to provide myself in this retreat with a store of cherries, or of grapes, according to the season; and really I should have spent there many hours of delicious day-dreaming, but for the irrepressible fits of remorse which troubled me so constantly — remorse for not doing my lessons.

Between the dropping garlands of leaves I could see, close by, the sparkling pool surrounded by lilliputian grottoes for which I had a sort of worship since my brother's departure. On its tiny surface, all dimpled by the little jet of water, the sunbeams danced and were reflected at an angle, to be lost in the green vault above me on the underside of the boughs, a gleaming shimmer that was never still.

This arbour was a peaceful and shady nook where I could persuade myself that I was really in the country; I could listen to the foreign birds twittering on the other side of the old walls, in the aviary belonging to Antoinette's mamma, and to the free birds too, the martins under the eaves, or the less pretentious sparrows in the gardens near.

Sometimes I would stretch myself at full length on the green bench, to stare up between the sprays of honeysuckle at the white clouds sailing across the blue sky. I studied the manners and customs of the mosquitoes, who clung all day to the nether-side of the leaves, quivering on their long legs. Or else I concentrated my captivated attention on the old wall behind, where dreadful tragedies took place in the insect world; cunning spiders suddenly rushing out of their holes to seize some poor little heedless insect — which I almost always rescued with a straw.

I had too — I forgot to mention — the society of an old cat I dearly loved, and called *Supremacy*, the faithful companion of my childhood.

Supremacy, knowing the hours when I was to be found there, would come stealthily in on the tiptoes, so to speak, of his velvet paws, but never jumped up on me till he had consulted me with an enquiring look. He was very ugly, poor beast, queerly patched with colour on one side of his face; then a disastrous accident had set his tail askew, broken it at a right angle. Thus he was the subject of Lucette's constant raillery, for had not she a dynasty of the loveliest Angora cats in endless succession? When I went to see her, after asking after every member of my family, she hardly ever failed to add, with an air of condescension which sent me into fits of laughing: "And that horror of a cat. He is well I hope, my dear child."

XXXII.

MEANWHILE my museum made great progress; I had been obliged to have more shelves put up. My grand-uncle whom I often went to see and who took an increasing interest in my taste for natural history, found among his collection of shells several duplicates of which he made me a present. With indefatigable kindness and patience he taught me the learned classifications of Cuvier, Linnæus, Lamarck and Bruguières; and I am amazed to remember how attentive I was.

On a little old desk, very old, which formed part of the furniture of my museum, I kept a copy-book in which, from his notes, I copied down for each shell, carefully numbered, the name of its species, genus, family and class, and then that of the place it had come from. And there, in the subdued light which fell on my table, and the silence of that little den, so high up, and lonely, and filled with objects brought from the uttermost ends of the earth or unfathomed depths of the sea, when my mind had wondered long over the changeful mystery of animal forms and the infinite variety of shells, with what deep emotion I would write down opposite the name of a *Pyrula* or a *Terebratula* such words as these — redolent of enchantment and sunshine: "Eastern coast of Africa;" "Coast of Guinea;" "Indian Ocean."

It was in this same little room that I remember experiencing one afternoon in March, one of the strangest symptoms of that craving for reaction which, at a later period, in hours of entire self-abandonment, was to drive me into the noise and tumult, the simple, animal joyousness of sailors.

It was Shrove Tuesday. I had been out in the sunshine with my father to see something of the masqueraders in the streets; then, having come in early, I had gone straight upstairs to amuse myself with my shells and my classification. But the distant shouts of the masks, and the rumble of their drums followed me into my learned retirement, bringing with them an intolerable melancholy. It was an impression of the same kind, only far more distressing, as that left by the chant of the old cake-woman when her voice died away down the narrow streets and ramparts on winter nights. It was perfect anguish, sudden and unexpected, but quite vague. In a dumb confused way I was distressed at feeling myself shut in, with dead, dry things only fit for old men, while out-of-doors the common boys of every age and size, and the sailors — greater boys still — were running, and jumping, and singing at the top of their voices and wearing penny masks over their faces. I had not the smallest wish to be with them, I need hardly say; I even realized the impossibility with disdain and disgust. And I wanted very much to be just where I was, to reduce the many-tinted family of the *Purpurïdae* to order — as the twenty-third of the *Gasteropoda*.

But all the same those people in the street troubled me strangely. And then, feeling so unhappy, I went down to find my mother and beseech her to come up and keep me company. Astonished at my request, for as a rule I invited no one into my sanctuary, and above all surprised at my look of distress, she at first said jestingly that it was ridiculous for a boy nearly ten years old — still she at once agreed to come and settled herself with me in my museum, her embroidery in her hand — almost uneasy at my desire.

But then, easy in my mind, warmed by her mere presence, I set to work again and thought no more of the masqueraders, only looking at the window from time to time to see against the pane the outline of her dear face, as the March day closed in.

XXXIII.

IT is not surprising that I no longer remember the process, whether slow or swift, by which my vocation to be a minister became the more militant purpose to be a missionary. It seems to me that it must have been at an earlier period; for as long as I can remember I had always been eager about Protestant missions, above all to Southern Africa, the land of the Basutos. And from my very babyhood I had been a subscriber to *Le Messager*, a monthly magazine, and the picture on the title-page had struck me at an early age. This picture I may certainly place at the head of the list of those I spoke of as making an impression in spite of drawing, colour, or perspective. It represented an impossible palm-tree, on the shore of the sea behind which an enormous sun was setting; and, at the foot of the tree, a young savage watching the advent, from the remotest horizon, of the vessel bringing the Good Tidings of Salvation. In the very earliest beginnings of myself, when, as I lay in my little feathered nest, the world as yet appeared to me shapeless and grey, this picture had filled my brain with dreams. I was now able to understand the childishness of the design and execution, but I was still under the charm of that huge sun half swallowed in the sea, and of the little missionship in full sail towards an unknown land.

So now, when I was questioned, I would reply: "I shall be a missionary." But I spoke in a bated tone, as one not very sure of his powers; and I knew too that no one believed me. My mother listened to the announcement with a sad smile; at first, because this was beyond what she asked of my faith; and afterwards, because she divined no doubt that it would not be that, but something else, more changeful, and for the present impossible to foresee quite clearly.

A missionary! This seemed to combine everything. — Distant voyages, an adventurous life of constant peril — but in the service of the Lord and his sacred cause. This, for a time, left my conscience at ease.

But having hit on this solution, I avoided allowing my mind to dwell on it for fear of discovering some fresh terror in it. But yes, the cold water of commonplace sermons, vain repetitions, and religious cant, still dripped on my early faith. On the other hand, my weariful fears of life and of the future increased daily; a leaden curtain hung across my darkened path, and I could not lift its heavy folds.

XXXIV.

IN what has gone before I have not said enough of *la Limoise*, the spot where I was first introduced to the things of nature. All my childhood is closely connected with that speck of earth, its old oak-woods, and its stony soil carpeted with wild thyme or heather. During ten or twelve glorious summers I spent all my Thursday half-holidays there, and dreamed of it moreover from one Thursday to the next, all through the dreary days of lessons.

In the month of May our friends the D***s removed to this country house, Lucette with them, to stay after the vintage till the first crisp days of October; and I was taken there regularly every Wednesday evening. Only to go there was to me a beginning of delights. Very seldom did we drive, for it was but four miles or so away, though it seemed to me so very remote, so utterly lost in the woods. It lay to the south towards the region of warmer lands; if it had been to the north the charm would, to me, have been less.

So every Wednesday evening, when the sun was low—the hour varying with the month—I set out for the country with Lucette's brother, a great boy of eighteen or twenty, who at that time seemed to me a man of ripe age. I kept step with him as nearly as I could, walking faster than when I was out with my father and sister; we went down through the low quarters of the town, all quiet now, past the old sailors' barracks whence the familiar sound of bugles and drums came up as far as my museum on days when the wind blew from the south; then we passed out through the fortifications by the oldest and most weather-beaten gate — a gate little used excepting by peasants and flocks, and came out at last on the road leading to the river.

About a mile of a perfectly straight avenue, bordered at that time by very old pollard trees, all yellow with lichen, and with all their branches, like hair, blown to the left by the sea breeze sweeping incessantly from the west, across the broad waste of fields along the coast.

To those persons who, having pre-conceived notions of landscape beauty, insist on the picturesque of a vignette — a brook flowing between trees with a mountain crowned by a castle — I confess that this flat road is very ugly. For my part, I think it exquisite, notwithstanding the level lines of the horizon. To right and left, nothing but stretches of pasture where herds of cattle wander and feed; and in front of us what looks like a wall bounding the meadows rather sadly, like a long rampart: this is the cliff ending the stony plain beyond the river which flows at its foot — the further shore, higher than this and different in character, but no less flat and monotonous. It is in this very monotony that the charm lies for me of our unappreciated coast; the calm uniformity of the lines is unbroken for long stretches, and profoundly restful.

In our whole neighbourhood that familiar road is indeed what I love best, probably because so many of my school-boy visions were built up on those flat distances, where I still seem to see them from time to time. Also, it is the only scene which has not been spoilt for me by factories, docks and railway stations. It is mine absolutely, without anyone suspecting it, or dreaming, in consequence, of disputing my possession.

The entire charm which the exterior world seems to possess for us, resides in ourselves, emanates from us, is diffused by us, — each one for himself of course,— and is only reflected back to us. But I did not learn young enough to believe in this familiar truism. Hence, in my earliest years, the whole charm was localized for me in the weather-worn walls and the honeysuckles of our back garden, in the sands of " our island," in level meadow-land or stony common. Afterwards, by scattering it broadcast I only succeeded in enchanting the spring. For alas! that land of my childhood — whither perhaps I shall return to die — has lost much of its breadth and colour in my eyes; it is only now and then, here and there, that I can revive the illusions of the past; and besides, as is but natural, I am haunted there by too crushing memories of all that is gone.

Well, I was saying that every Wednesday evening I took that road with a light step to make my way towards the rocky cliff which closed in the pasture land, that region of oaks and boulders where *la Limoise* was situated, and which my imagination at that time magnified enormously. The river, which we had to cross, lay at the end of that straight avenue of gnarled trees in their dress of golden lichen, wrung and tossed by the west wind. The river itself was very uncertain, the sport of tides and of the caprices of the ocean. We could cross in a ferryboat or in a yawl, navigated by the same men whom I had always known, old sailors with faces blackened and beards bleached by the sun.

On the further shore, the land of stones, I seemed all at once to have left the town far, far behind me. Its grey walls were still in sight, but to my small wit distance increased by jerks and became suddenly remote. Everything about me, to be sure, was quite different: the soil, the wild flowers, the grasses, and the butterflies which flitted over them. Nothing here was the same as in the marshes and meadows about the town where I took my walks on other days of the week. And these differences, which others would not have noticed, could not fail to strike and delight me, accustomed as I was to waste my time in such minute observation of the minutest objects of nature and to lose myself in the contemplation of the tiniest mosses. The very twilights of those Wednesdays had something peculiar about them which I could not account for; the sun was generally setting just when we reached the further shore, and seen from the higher ground, the lonely plateau on which we stood, it seemed to me larger than usual as its red disk was swallowed up behind the fields of tall hay-grass which we had left behind us.

Having thus crossed the river we immediately quitted the high road, and followed the almost imperceptible paths which crossed a region, odiously profaned, alas! in those days, but then most exquisite, called *les Chaumes*.

This was a tract of common land belonging to the village, the antique spire of whose church appeared in the distance. Being public property it remained comparatively wild. A sort of plateau composed of a floor of rock slightly undulating and covered as with a carpet of short, dry, sweetly-smelling plants which crackled under foot; a whole world of tiny butterflies and quaintly-coloured microscopic beetles lived among the scarce little flowers.

Occasionally we came across a flock of sheep, and the shepherdesses who looked after them were much more countrified and sunburnt than those who lived nearer the town. And this melancholy common, all burnt with the sun, was to me the vestibule of *la Limoise;* it already had the smell of wild thyme and marjoram.

At the end of this little moor was the hamlet of Frelin, — I was fond of that name of Frelin. I always thought it was derived from those great hornets (frelons) in the woods of *la Limoise*, which built their nests in the hearts of certain oak-trees and which were destroyed in the spring by making great fires round them. The hamlet was composed of three or four cottages; low, as is the custom in our country, and old, grey with age; there were Gothic finials over the little round doorways and coats of arms half effaced. The glimpse I caught of them, almost always at the same hour and in the fading light, conjured up in my mind the mystery of the past; above all they demonstrated the antiquity of this rocky soil, far earlier than the fields round our town which have been reclaimed from the sea, and where nothing is much older than the time of Louis XIV.

After *le Frelin*, I began to look ahead along

the little paths where, as a rule, I very soon spied Lucette, coming to meet us, either walking or driving with her father or mother; and directly I saw her I ran forward to greet her.

We passed through the village and skirted the walls of the church, a marvellous little building of the twelfth century, in the rarest and very ancient Romanesque style;—then in the twilight which had been fast fading, a dark band seemed to rise before one: the forest of Limoise almost entirely composed of oaks with their dark thick foliage. Soon we were walking in the private roads of the estate, and passed the well where the thirsty oxen patiently waited their turn to drink. At last the little gate was reached and opened, and we entered the turfed court-yard, already plunged into darkness by the shadows of the century-old trees. The house was built between this court-yard and a garden left to run wild which bordered on the wood.

In entering the old rooms, with their white-washed walls and ancient wood-work, the first thing I sought was my butterfly net, which hung on the wall, always in the same place, ready for the hunt of the morrow.

After dinner, the evening was usually spent seated at the end of the garden on the benches in an arbour with its back against the fence, — its back turned on the unknown of the darkness beyond out of which came the hooting of the owls. And while we were there, in the beautiful, warm night, with bright stars overhead and the silence full of the chirping of crickets, suddenly a bell began to toll, very distant but very clear, down in the village church.

Oh! the *Angelus* of Echillais, heard in that garden in the beautiful evenings of days gone by! Oh! the sound of that bell, a little cracked, but silvery still, like those voices of some very old people, which have been pretty and still remain sweet! What a charm of the past, of calm devotion and peaceful death that sound diffused in the limpid darkness of the country! . . . And the bell rang on, in the distance, sometimes nearer, sometimes farther, as the sound was wafted to and fro by the warm breaths of air. I thought of all the people who must be listening to it in the lonely farms around, and I thought of all the deserted spots near, where there was no one to hear it, and shuddered as I thought of the wood so close at hand, in which the last vibrations died away.

A municipal council, composed of superior minds, after having tricked-out the old belfry with a flagstaff and a tri-colour flag, finally suppressed the *Angelus*. So there is an end of it; no one will now, in the summer evening, hear that time-honoured call. . . .

After that, how cheerful it was to go to bed, with the next day in prospect, Thursday, when one could amuse oneself all day. I should very likely have been frightened in the guest-chambers which were on the ground-floor of the big solitary house; so until I was twelve years old I was put upstairs in Lucette's mother's big bedroom, behind some screens which made me a little room of my own.

In my little corner was a glass book-case filled with books on navigation of the last century, mariners' log-books which had not been opened for a hundred years. And on the whitewashed walls there were every summer the same imperceptible little moths which flew in at the open windows in the daytime and slept there with outspread wings. Then there were some incidents which completed the evening's amusement, which always happened unexpectedly just as we were going to sleep: An unseasonable bat who made his entrance and flew madly round and round the lights, or an enormous buzzing moth which had to be chased out with a turk's head broom. Sometimes a storm broke loose, stirring up the trees which rattled their branches against the wall; bursting open the old windows which had been carefully closed, disturbing everything. I have a vivid recollection of those fearful and magnificent storms of *la Limoise* as they appeared to me in those days when everything was grander and larger than it is nowadays, and throbbed with a greater intensity of existence.

XXXV.

IT was about that time as far as I can remember — when I was nearly eleven — that the apparition rises of another little friend who was soon to be in high infantine favour with me — (Antoinette had left the country; Véronique was forgotten.)

She was called Jeanne and belonged to a family of naval officers who, like the D***s, had been connected with our own for more than a century. Her elder by two or three years, I had not at first taken any notice of her, thinking her too much of a baby no doubt.

To begin with, she had such a puny kitten-like face; it was impossible to foresee what the too tiny features might become, to say whether she would turn out pretty or ugly; then soon she acquired a certain winning grace, and by the time she was eight or ten years old had developed into a charming, darling little girl. Very full of fun and as sociable as I was shy; and as she went to many dances and children's parties to which I never went, she seemed to me the acme of fashionable elegance and correctness.

In spite of the intimacy between our two families it was obvious that her parents looked askance at our growing friendship, perhaps not approving of her having a boy for a companion. I was very much hurt at this, and so vivid are our childish impressions, that it took years, — indeed I was almost a young man, before I could forgive her father and mother the slights I then felt.

In consequence, I felt a growing desire to be allowed to play with her, and she, seeing this, assumed the part of the inaccessible little princess of the fairy tales, laughed mercilessly at my shyness, my awkward way of holding myself, my blundering entrance into the drawing-room; there was a constant passage of arms between us, or an endless exchange of priceless compliments.

When I was invited to pass the day with her, I enjoyed it very much in anticipation, but I had many mortifications afterwards, for I was always doing something stupid in the presence of people who did not understand me. And whenever I wanted her to come and dine with me it had to be carefully negotiated by my grand-aunt Bertha who was a person of authority in their eyes.

One day, when she came back from Paris, little Jeanne delighted me with an account of the fairy tale of *Peau d'Ane*,* which she had seen acted.

Her time, at any rate, was not thrown away, for *Peau d'Ane* was destined for four or five years to take up many hours, more precious than any I have wasted since.

Together we formed the splendid idea of mounting it on a little theatre which I possessed. This undertaking threw us together. — And little by little the project assumed in our heads the most gigantic proportions; it grew and grew, from month to month, as our powers of execution perfected themselves. We painted fantastic scenery, we dressed numberless little dolls for the proces-

---

* A popular fairy tale in which a princess is disguised in an ass's skin.

sions. Indeed, I shall often recur to this fairy tale which was one of the principal features of my childhood.

And even after Jeanne was tired of it, I went on with it alone, out-doing myself, launching out into grand enterprises, moonlight effects, illuminations, storms. I also made marvellous palaces, and gardens worthy of Aladdin. All the dreams of enchanted dwellings, and of foreign luxury which I realized, more or less, at a later time in different corners of the globe, had their origin for the first time on the little stage in this fairy tale: as I emerged from my mysterious beginnings, I might almost say that all the chimera of my life was first tried, put into action on that tiny stage. I must have been fifteen when the last scenes, still unfinished, were consigned forever to the cardboard boxes which still serve as their silent tomb.

And since I am anticipating the future, I may as well say the final word on this subject: during the last few years, now Jeanne has grown into a beautiful woman, we have twenty times talked of opening together the boxes where our little dead dolls are sleeping,—but we live so fast in the present day, that we have never yet found time, and never shall.

Our children, perhaps, some day—or, who knows, our grandchildren! In some future age when we are forgotten, our unknown successors, rummaging at the bottom of the mysterious cupboards, will make the extraordinary discovery of hosts of little people, nymphs, fairies and genii dressed by our hands.

XXXVI.

IT appears that certain children who live far inland, have an intense longing to see the sea. I, who had never quitted our monotonous plains, craved for a sight of the mountains. I pictured to myself as best I could, what they must be like; I had seen some in pictures, I had even painted them myself in the scenery of *Peau d'Ane*. My sister, during her travels in the neighbourhood of Lucerne, had sent me descriptions of them, had written me long letters about them, such as are not usually written to children at the age I then was. And my ideas had been further enlarged by some photographs of some glaciers which she had brought me for my stereoscope. But I ardently wished to see them with my own eyes. One day, as if in answer to my wishes, an eventful letter came. It was from a first cousin of my father's; they had been brought up together as brothers, but, for what reason I know not, nothing had been heard of him for thirty years. When I was born, they had already given up talking about him, consequently I had never heard of his existence. And it was he who wrote, begging that the old friendship might be renewed: he lived, he said, in a little southern town, buried among mountains; he also announced that he had some sons and a daughter of the respective ages of my brother and sister. His letter was very affectionate and the reply was in the same strain, telling him of our existence.

Then, the correspondence having continued, it was decided that I should go there with my sister to spend the holidays, and that she should fill a mother's place to me as when we went to the island.

The South, the mountains, this sudden widening of my horizon — and also these new cousins fallen from the skies, became the constant subject of my thoughts till the month of August, which was the time fixed for our departure.

XXXVII.

LITTLE Jeanne had been spending the day with me; it was the end of May, during that same spring of expectation, and I was twelve years old. All the afternoon we had been rehearsing our little jointed china dolls, five or six centimetres high; we had painted some of the scenery, we had been working at *Peau d'Ane*, in short, in the midst of a fine mess of paints, brushes, cuttings of card-board, gilt paper and scraps of gauze. Then when the time came to go down into the dining-room, we put all our precious work into a large box, which from that day, was sacred to that use and of which the inside, made of new deal, had a strong smell of pine resin.

After dinner, in the long peaceful twilight, we were taken for a walk together. But out of doors it was unexpectedly chilly — and this of itself saddened me to begin with — and the spring sky had a haze over it, which reminded me of winter. Instead of taking us out of the town, into the avenues and roads always gay with promenaders, we wended our way towards the big garden of the Marina, a more select spot, but always deserted after sunset.

On our way there, down a long straight street where not a soul was to be seen, as we passed the chapel of the Orphanage, we heard bells ringing and service going on for the " Month of Mary;" then a procession came out; little girls dressed in white, who seemed to shiver in their May muslins.

After taking a turn round the deserted quarter, and chanting a melancholy hymn, the modest procession, with its two or three banners, withdrew silently; nobody in the street had taken any notice of it; from one end to the other, we were the sole occupants; a feeling came over me that no one in the grey sky had noticed it either, that that too was empty. The poor little procession of forsaken children had touched my heart, and added to my disenchantment of May evenings the consciousness of the vanity of prayer and the nothingness of all things.

In the garden of the Marina, my sadness increased. It was decidedly cold, and to our surprise we actually shivered in our spring attire. Added to which there was not a single creature in sight. The big chestnuts in flower, the trees with their crowd of young leaves, fresh and bright, stood side by side in close array, absolutely alone; the magnificence of their verdure was spread out for no one to look at under an unchanging sky of cold, pale grey. In the flower-beds were a profusion of roses, peonies and lilies, which seemed to have mistaken the season, and to shiver as we did with the sudden chill of the twilight.

I have often found the melancholy of spring-time far greater than that of autumn; doubtless because it is all wrong, a deception in the one thing in the world which ought never to be a failure.

Being put out by all these things I was moved to play a school-boy trick on Jeanne.

I was sometimes tempted to do this to pay her out for being cleverer and forwarder than myself. I persuaded her to smell quite close to some charming lilies, and while she leaned over them, by a slight push at the back of her head I buried her nose in the flowers and covered it with yellow pollen. She was naturally indignant, and the knowledge that I had committed an uncourteous act, spoiled the rest of the walk home.

The beautiful evenings of May!... I had nevertheless a recollection of pleasant ones in preceding years; and were they like this?... This cold, this lowering sky, these solitary gardens? And this day of amusement with Jeanne so soon over, so badly ended! Inwardly I concluded with the deadly: "Is that all?" which became later one of my commonest reflections; I might as well have taken it for my motto. When I got home, I went to look at the result of our afternoon's work in the wooden chest, and I smelt the aromatic odour of the deal boards which had scented all our theatrical properties. Well, for a long time, for a year, two years or more, that same smell of the chest of *Peau d'Ane* brought vividly back to me that May evening and its intense sadness, which was one of the most singular experiences of my young life. However, as a man I have never gone through those spasms of anguish from no recognizable cause with their undercurrent of misery at not understanding, at feeling that I had lost my footing always in the same unfathomable abyss.

I have hardly ever suffered since without, at any rate, knowing why. No, those things were peculiar to my childhood, and this book might as well have borne the title (a dangerous one I grant you): "Journal of my unexplained sorrows, and of the tricks by which occasionally I sought to forget them."

XXXVIII.

IT was about this same time that I took possession of my Aunt Claire's room, for preparing my lessons and working at *Peau d'Ane*. I settled myself in it as a conqueror in a vanquished country, spreading my things about everywhere, the thought of being in the way never occurring to me.

In the first place, Aunt Claire was the person who indulged me most. Then she was so careful with all my treasures. If I had taken out any fragile things, things that the slightest draught would blow away, for instance, butterflies or beetles' wings to decorate the costumes of my nymphs and fairies — I had but to say to her, "dear Aunt, I trust to you looking after them," I could be quite easy in my mind, and go and leave them, sure that no one would touch them.

One of the chief attractions of that room was the bear which contained sugar almonds; I sometimes went in for the sole purpose of paying him a visit. He was made of china and seated on his hind legs, resided on a corner of the mantel-piece. It was understood between Aunt Claire and me, that whenever his head was turned on one side (and it was often so turned, three or four times in the course of the day), that there was a burnt-almond or other sugar-plum awaiting me. When I had eaten it I carefully put his head on straight, to show I had been there, and went away. Aunt Claire, too, helped with *Peau d'Ane;* she worked at the dresses, and every day I set her a task. She had especially undertaken the head-dresses of the nymphs and fairies; on their china heads, no bigger than the top of one's little finger, she fixed blond silken wigs, which she afterwards curled in scattered ringlets, by means of imperceptible curling pins.

Then, when I made up my mind to learn my lessons, in the last feverish half-hour, having wasted my time in all sorts of idleness, it was

Aunt Claire again who came to my assistance. She took charge of the big dictionary and looked up my words for my exercises and translations. She had even taught herself to read Greek, in order to help me to learn my lessons in that language. For that study I dragged her out on the stair-case, where I spread myself out on the steps, my feet higher than my head: for two or three years following, this was my classic attitude during the repetition of the Cyropædia or the Iliad.

XXXIX.

IT was a real joy when a storm broke over *la Limoise* on a Thursday evening, and prevented my returning home.

On more than one occasion it has been known to occur. I could therefore buoy myself up with this hope on the days I had not finished my tasks . . . (For a pitiless professor had inaugurated Thursday tasks; I was now obliged to drag down books and copy-books with me; my poor days in the open air were quite darkened by them.)

It happened one evening that the longed-for storm had come with splendid violence, and at about eight o'clock Lucette and I, both a little alarmed, were together in the big solemn drawing-room, its bare walls decorated with only two or three quaint old pictures in old-fashioned frames; she putting the last touches to a piece of work under her mother's eye; I playing softly a dance tune of Rameau's on the antiquated country piano, and finding much pleasure in the old-world music thus strangely mingled with the dull roar of the thunder-claps.

The work being finished, Lucette turned over the pages of my copy-books which were lying about on the table, and at one glance ascertained that I had not done any work, suddenly she said to me: "Where have you put your Duruy's *History?*"

My Duruy's *History?* ... Where on earth could the book be? A new book with hardly any ink spots on it yet... —Oh! my Goodness! out there, forgotten, at the end of the garden, in the furthest asparagus-bed!... (For my historical studies, I frequented one of the asparagus-beds, which were turned in summer into a sort of glade, of high, feathery, green grass; whilst a certain hazel copse, thick, impenetrable, and as dark as a green cavern, was the chosen spot for the far more difficult work of writing Latin verses.) This time I was well scolded by Lucette's mother, and it was decided to go at once to the rescue of the book.

The expedition was organized: In front walked a man-servant carrying a stable lantern; behind him Lucette and I, in sabots, held up with great difficulty, the umbrella which the storm incessantly turned inside out.

Out of doors I no longer felt alarmed; but I opened my eyes wide and listened with all my ears. Oh! how wonderful and sinister the end of the garden appeared, seen in the lurid glare of the green flashes, which trembled and quivered, and from time to time, left us blinded in the darkness.

And what an impression the oak wood made on me, as from its depths came now and again the crash of falling branches. . . .

In the asparagus-bed, we found, soaked and caked with mud, my Duruy's *History*. Before the storm, the snails, no doubt, made lively by the approach of rain, had walked all over it, and drawn fantastic patterns in the glistening slime.

Well, those snail tracks on the book remained there for a long time preserved by my care under a paper cover. They had a charmed gift of reminding me of a thousand things owing to the power of association which always existed in my brain between the most dissimilar ideas if only once they had had any connection of mere happy coincidence. These little shining zigzags on the cover of the book, seen by candle-light called up at once the air by Rameau, the thin tones of the piano, and above them the roll of the storm; they brought before my eyes a scene, suggested to me that very evening, by a print from Teniers hanging on the wall, of little last-century figures dancing in the shade of woods like those of *la*

Limoise; they revived a complete vision, as it had then appeared to me of pastoral amusements in the old time under old oak groves.

XL.

AND yet the home-coming on Thursday evening would sometimes have been very delightful but for my remorse over those never-done tasks. We went as far as the river in the carriage, or I rode the donkey, or we walked. As soon as we had turned our backs on the stony plateau of the southern bank and crossed the river, I always found my father and sister waiting for me, and with them I merrily set out along the straight road to the town, between the flat fields. I trotted on at a good pace in my glee at seeing my mother and the aunts and dear home.

By the time we went in at the old town-gate it was quite dark — a spring or a summer night. As we passed the sailor's barracks we could hear the familiar bugle call and beat of drum proclaiming the early bed-time for the men.

Then in our own home, it was generally at the end of the garden, that I found the dear black gowns, sitting out under the stars or in the arbour of honeysuckles. Even if the others had gone in I was sure of finding Aunt Bertha there alone — independent by nature she defied evening chills and the falling dew; and after kissing me she would sniff my clothes to make me laugh, and exclaim: "Yes — you smell of *la Limoise*."

Very true — so I did. On coming from thence all my things had a fragrance of wild thyme and herbs and sheep; an aromatic flavour peculiar to that spot of earth.

XLI.

IN speaking of *la Limoise* I must be vain enough to tell the story of a thing I did which was really heroic as an act of obedience and fidelity to my promise. It occurred a short while before our departure for the South, which so filled my imagination; it was in the month of July next after my twelfth birthday.

On a certain Wednesday, having been sent off rather earlier than usual to make sure of my arriving before dark, at my earnest entreaty I was escorted no further than to the gate of the town, and then, for a treat, I was allowed to go alone to *la Limoise* like a big boy.

On crossing the river I pulled out of my pocket with unutterable shamefacedness before those seabeaten old sailors, a white silk neckerchief which I had promised to tie round my throat as a precaution against cold on the water. And then having to cross the common, a shadeless region always scorched by a burning sun, I fulfilled the pledge I had given at home — I opened a sunshade. Oh! How I felt myself blushing, how bitterly ridiculous when I passed a little sheperdess minding her sheep. To crown all, coming out of the village I met four boys, on their way home from school, no doubt, who even from afar stared at me in amazement. Good Heavens! I felt my courage failing — could I really keep my word till the end?

They came close by me, peeping under my hat to see a boy who was so much afraid of the sunshine; and one of them made this senseless remark which made me tingle as much as a mortal insult: "It is the Marquis of Carabas!" and they all began to laugh. However, I went on my way without flinching or replying, though the blood was scorching in my cheeks and humming in my ears, and I kept my sunshade up!

In the course of my life, it has often been my fate to have insults flung at me by common people ignorant of the meaning of things, and to take no notice; but I never remember being annoyed by them. But this scene! No. My conscience never again led me to perform so meritorious an act.

And I am perfectly convinced that this incident and nothing else gave rise to the aversion for an umbrella which has haunted me through life. I ascribe, too, to the comforters and padding and excessive care generally, to which I was then a victim, the craving which came over me at the age of reactionary extremes to tan my chest in the sun and bare it to all the winds of heaven.

XLII.

WITH my head hanging out of window as the train rushed on, I kept asking my sister who filled the opposite seat:

"Are not those the mountains?"

"Not yet," she would say, having the Alps in her mind. "Not yet. High hills at most."

It was an August day, hot and splendid. An express train was bearing us southwards; we were on our way to the unknown cousins.

"But there — look there?" cried I in triumph, gazing with wide open eyes at something higher than all else, a blue shape on the clear horizon.

She leaned out. "Ah, yes," said she. "This time I grant you. — They are not very high, but still. . . ."

Everything was a delight to us that evening,

at the hotel in a town where we were obliged to stay till the morrow; and I remember the glorious night that fell while we stood with our elbows on the rail of our balcony watching the blue mountains grow dark, and listening to the chirp of the grasshoppers.

Next day, the third of our journey, which had been divided into stages, we hired a funny little vehicle to convey us to the little town — then quite out of the world — where our relations dwelt. Through narrow gorges and ravines and across bridges we had five hours, which to me were perfect enchantment. Besides the mere fact of the mountains, every little thing was new and strange; the soil and stones were vivid red; instead of our hamlets always so white with snowy lime-wash, and always so uniformly low, as though they dared not lift their heads above the vast level of the plain, here the houses, like the rocks, were ruddy and uplifted quaint gables and old turrets, high, very high up on the ridges of the hills. The peasants were brown-skinned and talked an unknown tongue, and the women especially attracted my attention, walking with a free balance unknown to our peasant women and carrying loads or sheaves on their head, or huge copper water-jars. My every faculty was awake and alert — perilously fascinated by this first revelation of foreign and unknown life.

Late in the day we reached the strange little town which was our destination, on the banks of one of those southern rivers which rush noisily over their shallow bed of white boulders. It still had its ancient arched gateways, its high machicolated ramparts, its streets of Gothic houses — and dull red was the general hue of all the buildings.

Somewhat puzzled and excited we looked about for these cousins whose faces were unknown to us even by portraits, and who, to be sure, would be on the look-out for us and have come to meet us. Suddenly we discerned a tall young fellow, and on his arm a girl in a white muslin dress; and at once, without the least hesitancy on either side, we exchanged tokens of recognition — we had found each other.

At their own door on the steps stood the parents to welcome us; both in advanced life, having still the traces of remarkable beauty. They had an old house dating from the time of Louis XIII, in the corner of one of those squares built round with porches, such as are often seen in our little southern country-towns. We went first into a hall paved with pinkish stone, where, on one side, there was an enormous copper cistern with a tap. A staircase of the same stone, very wide and with curious balustrades of wrought iron, led up to the old panelled rooms on the first floor. And at once I felt that the past to which these things belonged was different from that of Saintonge and the island — the only part with which as yet I was at all familiar.

After dinner we all went to sit by the brawling river, in a meadow among centaury and marjoram which even in the dark we knew by their penetrating scent. It was very hot, very still, and myriads of crickets were chirping. I fancied I never had before seen a night so translucent, or so many stars crowded into so deep a blue. The difference in latitude was not, indeed, very great, but the sea-breezes, which make our winters mild, cast a haze over our summer-nights, so this sky was very likely clearer than that at home, more southern.

All round, we were shut in by grey blue shapes rising into the air, and which I could never tire of gazing at. The mountains which I had never seen gave me that sense of abroadness I had so longed to feel, showing me that my first dream was indeed fulfilled.

It was my fate to spend several summers in this little town and to become so familiar with it as to be able to speak the dialect of the good people of the place. The two homes of my childhood were in fact Saintonge and this southern spot, both were warmed with sunshine.

As for Brittany, which many persons suppose to be my birthplace, I never saw it till long after, when I was seventeen, and it was long before I loved it — the reason, perhaps, why I loved it more. At first it weighed on me with depressing sadness; it was my brother Ives who first initiated me into its melancholy charm and made me at home in its cottages and in its timber-built chapels. And, finally, the influence exerted on my imagination by a young girl of the Tréguier district at a much later date, when I was about seven and twenty made me really love this adopted home.

XLIII.

ON the day after my arrival at our southern Cousins' I was introduced to some new play-fellows: the little Peyrals, who, after the manner of the country, had the article always prefixed to their names; they were *la Maricette* and *la Titi*, two little girls of ten and eleven — my companions were still little girls — and *le Médou*, a younger brother, almost a baby, who did not count. As I was on the whole very young for a boy of twelve — in spite of certain intuitions as to matters outside the ken, as a rule, of most children — we at once formed a most sympathetic little party, and our friendship persisted through several summers.

The father of these little Peyrals was the owner of woods and vineyards on the hillsides, where we reigned supreme; no one interfered with our schemes, not even the most absurd. In this perfectly remote country-village, where our families were held in such high respect by the peasantry, it was supposed that we could come to no harm in our wanderings. So we set off, all four of us, early in the day for a picnic dinner in some distant vineyard, or in pursuit of undiscoverable butterflies, sometimes enlisting any little peasant children we met, for they were always ready to follow us submissively, and such freedom as this after the incessant watchfulness to which I had hitherto been accustomed, was to me a delightful change. A new life of independence and open air began for me among the mountains; but I might almost say it was a continuation of my isolation, for I was the eldest of the party and led them in my very fantastic games. Intellectually— in the realm of dreams, there were wide gulfs between us. I was the undisputed head of the tribe; only Titi now and then rebelled and was immediately pacified; their one idea was, very sweetly, to please me, and it suited me very well to have the upper hand. This was the first time I had been a leader. I had other troops of followers in my amusements at a later time, and less easy to manage; but I always liked best that they should consist of my juniors — younger than myself in intelligence especially, and more simple-minded, neither interfering with my caprices, nor — above all — laughing at my childishness.

XLIV.

AS a holiday task I had merely been desired to read *Télémaque* — my education, it will be observed, had some old-world features. It was in a little eighteenth century edition, in several volumes. And, wonderful to say, it did not particularly bore me; I had a clear vision of Greece and its white marbles under a pure blue sky; and my spirit unfolded itself to a conception of antiquity which was, no doubt, much more pagan than Fénelon's: Calypso and her nymphs enchanted me.

To do my reading I withdrew from the little Peyrals for a few minutes every day, to one or another of two favorite nooks: the garden or the loft.

This enormous loft, under the tall Louis XIII. roof, extended for the whole length of the house, the windows were always shuttered and the place always dark. Old relics of a past time sleeping up there under the dust and spider webs had attracted me from the first; and then I had got into the habit of stealing up there with my *Télémaque*, after the mid-day dinner, sure that no one would look for me there. At that hour of scorching sunshine it was by comparison quite dark. I noiselessly set a shutter ajar, letting in a flood of blinding light. Then leaning out over the roof I rested my elbows on the hot old slates seamed with golden mosses, and read at my ease. Within reach of my hand thousands of Agen plums lay drying for winter use, spread out on reed mats; baked in the sun through and through, they were perfectly delicious; the whole loft was fragrant with them, and the bees and wasps which feasted on them as I did tumbled about on their backs surfeited with sweets and heat. And on every roof in the neighbourhood, among the ancient Gothic gables, similar reed mats were spread, as far as I could see, covered with just such plums and haunted by buzzing insects.

I could also see from thence in sloping perspective the two streets which met at the corner formed by my cousins' house. The long rows of mediæval houses ended, in each, in a Gothic gateway in the high town-wall of red stone. The town was torpid, and hot, and silent in the hush of summer noon; not a sound was heard but the cackle of innumerable fowls and ducks, pecking the sun-dried rubbish in the streets below.

I took my *Télémaque* in very small doses; three or four pages satisfied my curiosity and set my conscience at ease for the rest of the day; then I made haste down again to join my little friends, and we set out for the vineyards or the woods.

The garden of which I spoke, whither I sometimes retired, was not attached to the house; like all the other gardens it lay outside the Gothic walls of the townlet. It was enclosed by rather high walls and the entrance was through a door with a round arch, locked with a gigantic key. Sometimes I would go off there alone with my *Télémaque* and my butterfly net.

There were plum-trees there from which those same delicious plums dropped, overripe, on the scorching soil; all along the old paths vines were pleached where legions of bees and flies devoured the scented grapes. And the further end lay waste — for it was very large — overgrown with lucerne like an open field.

The charm of this old orchard was the feeling of solitude, of being locked in perfectly alone in the wide space and the silence.

I must also mention a certain arbour which was there, in which two years later the crowning event of my child-life occurred. It was backed by the outer wall, and covered by a trellice and vine always baking in the sun. This place gave me, I know not precisely why, an impression of the tropics. — And in truth in our colonial garden-plots I really did find, at a later date, the same heavy scent and general aspect of things. This arbour was the occasional haunt of a rare kind of butterflies which I never found elsewhere; looked at from the front they were simply yellow and black, but a side glance showed them gorgeous with blue metallic lustre, just like those foreigners from Guiana which were to be seen, with pins through them, in my museum — uncle's glass boxes. They were very distrustful and difficult to catch, hovering for an instant over the musk-scented grapes and then flitting away over the wall. Then setting my toes in the breaches of the wall, I dragged myself to the top to watch them disappear across the slumbering, silent country, and would rest there some time leaning on my elbows and contemplating the distance. All round me rose the wooded mountains, with here and there the ruins of a castle of feudal towers on a height;

and in the foreground, surrounded by fields of maize and buckwheat, I saw the *Domain of Bories* with its old vaulted porch; the only house in the neighbourhood which was whitewashed, like the entrance to an African town.

This place I was told, belonged to some children named Sainte-Hermangarde, who were to come soon and to be my playfellows; but I almost dreaded their advent, so thoroughly was I satisfied with the society of the little Peyrals.

XLV.

CASTELNAU! This ancient name calls up for me images of sunshine of pure light on high hills, of calm melancholy among ruins, of devout meditation in the face of departed splendours, buried for ages.

This old castle of Castelnau was perched on one of the neighbouring wooded heights, the russet pile of its terraces and ramparts, its towers and turrets standing out against the sky. It could be seen from my cousin's old garden, its distant head peeping above the wall.

It was indeed the most conspicuous object in the landscape for miles round, the one thing it was impossible to avoid seeing, the crenelated ridge of red masonry, rising up from among a dense clump of trees, a ruin set like a crown on a pedestal overgrown with the verdure of chestnuts and oaks. On the first day of my arrival I had caught sight of it at once, both surprised and attracted at this ancient eagle's nest, which in those dark middle ages must have been so grand. And as it happened, it was a custom in the summer for all my cousin's family to go up two or three times a month, to spend the day and dine with the owner —an old priest who lived in a comfortable little house hanging on to the ruins.

Those were days of joy and fairy dreams for me.

We set out, all together, early enough to have crossed the plain before the hottest hours of the day. As soon as we reached the foot of the mountain we felt the cool shade of the forest which was wrapped in a grand mantle of green. Then, under the vault of huge oaks and thick foliage we went up, up, by a zigzag path, all the family on foot in single file, a serpentine procession like the pilgrims wending their way to the solitary abbeys on cliffs in Gustave Doré's mediæval landscapes. Here and there from under the ferns a tiny spring oozed out and trickled in a channel across the red soil; between the trees deep vistas peeped through the gaps. At last, on reaching the top, we were in the strangest and most old-world village, perched up there for ages; and we rang at the priest's little gate. His house and garden-plot were overhung by the castle with its chaos of red walls and towers, crumbling, riven and falling. The deepest peace seemed to emanate from this ruined eyrie, it breathed an immense silence, which lay, awful, on everything near.

Very long were the dinners the good old priest used to give us; not unfrequently one of those southern "feeds" to which the notabilities of the neighbourhood were invited. Ten or fifteen dishes, one after another, with the choicest golden fruits and wines of the best vintages of that country, then so richly productive. So we sat at table hour after hour in those hot August or September afternoons, and I, the only child of the party, could not endure it; haunted by the overpowering sense of the adjoining ruins, at the second course I asked leave to depart. Then an old woman would come out with me and open the outer door of the feudal walls of Castelnau; then she placed the keys of the immense place in my hands and I went on alone with delicious trepidations, knowing the way well enough through gates with drawbridges and up towering ramparts.

Here I was then, alone for a long time, sure that no one would come after me for an hour or two; free to wander about this labyrinth, master in these high and melancholy precincts. Oh! The dreams I have had there! — First I went round all the terraces overhanging the woods I looked down into; infinite distances spread on every side of me, here and there in the distance rivers laced the scene with silver, and through the translucent summer-atmosphere I could see across to the neighbouring province. A great calm seemed to reign in this corner of France which lived its own little life, somewhat as in a bygone time, unvisited as yet by any railway line.

Then I went into the interior of the ruin — the courtyards, the stairs, the deserted passages; I climbed up into the towers, scaring flocks of pigeons, or rousing bats and owls from their noonday slumbers. On the first floor there were suites of huge rooms, not yet unroofed, and very dark with closed shutters; where I used to wander in an ecstasy of fear, listening to the sound of my own steps in that sepulchral emptiness, studying the strange Gothic painting, and faded frescoes, or still faintly-gilt ornaments — monsters and garlands of impossible flowers, added at the Renaissance; the whole telling of a past which rose up before me, wildly fantastic and savagely magnificent, dim in a remote distance, and yet bright with the same southern sunshine as was now baking these deserted red stone walls. Even now, when I can see Castelnau in a true light, looking at it in memory with eyes, which have seen something of all that is most splendid on earth, I still think of that Enchanted Castle of my childhood as being, with its beautiful situation, one of the most sumptuous relics of feudal France.

In one tower there was a certain room with a coffered ceiling in royal blue powdered with rosettes and badges in gold. — Nothing has ever given me such an intimate sense of mediævalism. In the midst of that silence as of the dead, with my elbows on the sill of a little window sunk in the thick wall, I gazed down on the green depths trying to picture to myself, on the roads so far below, cavalcades of men-at-arms, or processions of knights and ladies. To me, brought up amid level plains, one of the strangest charms of the place was the wide vacant blue of the distance which peeped through every crack, or loophole, or opening of any kind in the halls and towers, and which at once gave me a sense new to my experience of being high, high, above the world.

XLVI.

LETTERS from my brother on that very thin paper and written very close, used to reach us at irregular intervals as sailing vessels happened to arrive that had been cruising out there on the Great Ocean. Some of them were to me, very long ones too, with never-to-be-forgotten descriptions. I already knew several words of the soft-sounding language of Oceania, and in my dreams at night I often saw the Delicious Isle and wandered there. It haunted my fancy like a Happy Valley, ardently longed for, but quite inaccessible, in another planet.

One of these letters, forwarded by my father, came to me while I was staying with these cousins in the south.

I went up to the roof of the loft to read it, on the sunny side where the plums were drying. He gave me a long account of a place called Fataüa, a deep ravine between two precipices: " perpetual twilight reigned there under tall, unfamiliar trees, and the spray of waterfalls kept the rarest ferns forever green." — Yes, I saw it all; and so much more clearly now that I, too, had mountains about me with damp dells full of ferns. The whole thing was described fully and completely; my brother had no suspicion of the dangerous witchery his letters already exercised over the child he had left so happy by the fireside, so quiet, so pious.

"The only pity," he added, "was that the Delicious Isle should not have some little back door opening into our garden — into the honeysuckle arbour, for instance, behind the little pond."

This notion of a door in the wall of our garden-plot, and above all the connection with the little pool which my far-away brother himself had made, struck me strangely, and the next night this was my dream:

I went into our garden. It was in a deadly twilight as if the sun had gone out forever; over everything and in the air there was the unutterable desolation of dreams which when we are awake we cannot even conceive of. At the end of the garden, by that beloved little pool, I felt myself rise from the earth like a bird taking flight. At first I was tossed to and fro like some very light creature, and then I floated over the wall to the southwest in the direction of Oceania; I had no wings that I could see, and I was lying on my back in an agony of giddiness and fear of falling; then I went on at a terrific speed, like a stone shot from a sling; the stars whirled madly about me in space; beneath me seas on seas were gliding away, pale and bewildering, and still in that twilight of a dying world. — Presently, suddenly, the great trees of the gorge of Fataüa were closing over me in the dark. I was there.

There, in that place I dreamed on; but I no longer believed in my dream — so completely was I aware of the impossibility of ever really being there. — Besides, I had too often been the dupe of such visions, which vanished with my slumbers. I only dreaded waking, so bewitched was I with this ineffectual illusion. The carpet of ferns was there; in the deep gloom I gathered them, feeling for them, and saying to myself: "These plants, at any rate, must be real, since I can touch them, and have them in my hand; they surely cannot disappear when I wake...." And I clutched them with all my might to be sure of holding them.

I woke. The beautiful summer's day was breaking; the clatter of life was beginning — the perpetual chick and crooning of the hens already pecking about the streets, and the rattle of the weavers' looms at once reminded me of where I was. My empty hand was still clenched, the nails almost set in the palm, to keep tight hold of the imaginary nosegay from Fataüa — the airy nothing of a dream.

XLVII.

I HAD very soon become attached to my grown-up cousins, and as familiar with them as though I had known them all my life. I fancy that only the tie of blood avails to create these immediate intimacies between persons who the day before did not know of each other's existence. I was very fond, too, of my uncle and aunt, as we called them; especially of my aunt who spoilt me a little and who was still very good and beautiful to behold, in spite of her sixty years and her grey hair, and her grandmotherly dress. She was a woman of a type which will soon be extinct in our day, when everything is being levelled and pared to one pattern. Born in the neighbourhood of her house, of a very old family, she had never quitted that province of France; her manners, her hospitality, her courtesy, had a local stamp, and that was a detail which attracted me.

In total contrast to my narrow, padded life at home, here I lived entirely out of doors, in the roads and the streets. And these streets were strange and delightful to me, paved with black cobbles, like the streets in the East, and overshadowed by old houses — Gothic, or of the Louis XIII period. The women who went past, too, peasant women with goitres, as they came in from the fields and vineyards, with baskets of fruit on their heads, always would stop to offer me the ripest grapes and most delicious peaches.

Then, too, I was delighted with the southern dialect, the mountaineers' songs, all the foreign aspect of things which came upon me from all sides at once. To this day, when I happen to cast my eye on some of the treasures I brought home for my little museum, or to come across one of the little letters I wrote every day to my mother, I seem suddenly to feel the sunshine, the new strangeness, the fruity fragrance of the South, the fresh mountain air — and I am conscious that in spite of my long descriptions these dead pages can reproduce nothing of it all.

XLVIII.

THE little Sainte-Hermangardes, of whom I had heard so much, arrived in the middle of September. Their home lay to the north, towards la Corrèze; and they came every year to spend the autumn in a rambling, dismantled old house, next door to my cousins'. This time there were boys; two boys rather older than I. But in spite of my fears I liked them at once. They were accustomed to live during a large part of the year in the remote country on their own estate, and they had guns and gunpowder; they went out shooting. Thus they brought quite a new element into my games. Their grounds at Bories became one of our centres of operations. Everything there was at our command — servants, beasts, and buildings. And one of our amusements now at the end of the holidays, was to make enormous paper balloons, which we inflated by burning hay under them, and then sent sailing away, high up, till they were lost in the fields or the trees.

But these children even were not quite like all others; they were brought up by a private tutor with different notions from those which prevail at a town-school. When there was any difference of opinion among us, each was ready to give way out of politeness; thus their society again, was ill-adapted to prepare me for the friction of life.

One day they came — it was very sweet of

them — to bring me a very rare butterfly, a variety of the sulphur-yellow which has on the front wings a lovely tinge of rosy orange, like the flush of dawn. It was at Bories, they told me, that they had caught it, and with so much care that there was not a finger-mark on its delicate tints. And just as they brought it, at noon, in the hall of the old house, which was always closely shut up during the day, to exclude the oppressive heat, my old cousin might be heard behind the scenes, singing in a thin, plaintive mountain falsetto. He was fond of pitching his voice in this tone, and at that moment it struck me with peculiar melancholy in the silent heat of the late September noon. And again and again it was the same old song: "*Ah! ah! la bonne histoire. . .*" which he began and never finished. So from that moment the house at Bories, the sulphur butterfly, and the doleful little tune of "*la bonne histoire,*" remained inseparably linked in my mind.

But, indeed, I am saying too much about these incoherent associations of images which I was so apt to form; this is the last time; I will do so

no more. But in the sequel it will be seen that **it was** important to record this one with reference **to what** follows.

XLIX.

WE returned home in the beginning of October.
But a disastrous event marked our return: I was sent to school — as a day-boy of course; and equally of course, I never was allowed to go or come alone for fear of mischief. My school-life, as it turned out, was limited to four years of day-schooling, the freest and most whimsical that can be imagined.

Nevertheless, from that fatal day my little story was very much spoilt.

School began at half-past two on one of those delicious days in October — warm and calmly sunny, which are like a sad farewell from the summer. It had been so lovely among the mountains, the leafless forests, the russet vines! I first entered on the scene of durance as one of a swarm of children all talking together. My first impression was one of surprise and disgust at the hideous bareness of the ink-splashed walls and the shiny old forms of worn wood, all patterned with penknife-carving, where at once one felt how many school-boys had been victimized. My new companions, though unknown to me, treated me with patronizing or impertinent familiarity from the first; I, on my side, gazed at them shyly, thinking them very rude, and for the most part, very dirty.

I was twelve and a half, and was placed in the third class; my home tutor having said that I was capable of the work if I took pains, though my little stock of knowledge was very unequal. That first day we all had to write a Latin exercise, to place us in the class, and I remember that my father was waiting for me himself, somewhat anxious as I came out of this trial-day. I told him I was second of fifteen, astonished at his attaching so much importance to a matter in which I took so little interest. It was quite the same to me. Heart-broken as I was how could I care for such a trifle?

And even later emulation remained unknown to me. To be at the bottom of his class always seemed to me the least of the evils a school-boy has to endure.

The weeks as they followed were utterly miserable. In fact, my intelligence shrank before the multiplicity of exercises and tasks; even my own little dreamland seemed to be fading into nothingness. The first fogs, the first grey days, added their desolate gloom to it all. The Savoyard sweeps had come back to the towns, with their autumnal cry, which in bygone years had touched my heart and moved me to tears. To children the approach of winter brings unreasonable forebodings of the end of all things, of death in cold and darkness; time seems so long at that age, that they fail to look foward to the revival which will come to all. It is not till we are well on in life, and ought on the contrary, to think more of the lapse of seasons, that we think of a winter as a mere trifle.

I had a calendar in which I marked off the days one by one. At the beginning of this year of school-life I felt quite crushed by the long perspective of months—interminable months, through which I must live before even the Easter holidays — a respite of a week from dulness and discomfort; I had no courage — sometimes I really sank into despair at the slow crawling lapse of time.

Ere long cold, bitter cold, came to aggravate matters. Oh! that arrival at school on December mornings, when for two mortal hours we had to sit in a room warmed by a smoky sea-coal fire, and when the icy wind in the streets must be faced to get home again. Other boys skipped and jumped, and knew how to make slides when the gutters were frozen. I knew none of these things, and they would have struck me as highly incorrect. I was escorted home, walking nicely and chilled to the marrow; humiliated too at being fetched, laughed at sometimes by the others, not popular with my class and somewhat disdainful of my fellow-captives, with whom I had not a single idea in common.

Then on Thursdays my tasks went on all day.

with "impositions"— ridiculous impositions — which I scrawled off in the vilest writing possible by the help of every school-boy trick — blotting off duplicates and tying pens five in a row. And in my disgust at life I did not even keep myself tidy; I was constantly in trouble for rough hair and dirty hands — ink-stained only of course. But if I were to go on I should make my narrative the mirror of all the deadly weariness of those days.

L.

"CAKES, cakes, nice cakes, all hot!" The worthy old woman had begun her evening walks again, her quick, shuffling pace and doleful tune. She hurried by at the same hour every day with the regularity of an automaton. And so the long winter evenings had come again, just like those of many years already past and of two or three yet to come. Every Sunday at eight o'clock the D***'s would arrive with Lucette, and some other neighbours with a very little girl named Marguerite, who had lately become intimate in the house. A new game had been devised for the close of these winter Sunday evenings, over which the thought of the morrow's lessons weighed more sadly than ever. After tea, when I knew that the end was near and that they would be going away, I carried off this little Marguerite into the dining-room and we set to running round and round the table like mad things, trying which could catch the other in a sort of frenzy. She was caught at once, of course, and I hardly ever; so she was always the pursuer, and most vehement; slapping the table, and shouting, and making a really infernal racket. By the time we had done, the rugs were turned up, the chairs out of place, everything topsy-turvy. We found it very dull — and I was indeed too old for such play. In point of fact there was nothing in the world more dismal to me than these final romps on Sunday, with the terror of Monday hanging over me and the weary round of tasks once more. It was merely a way of prolonging *in extremis* this day of truce; of stunning my woes by sheer noise. It was a sort of challenge flung in the face, as it were, of those never-done tasks, which were a burden to my conscience and would presently trouble my dreams, which I must scramble through somehow next morning in my bed-room, by candle-light or in the dim frozen dawn, before the hateful hour of school once more.

The family in the drawing-room were, to be sure, somewhat dismayed at hearing this bacchanalian riot; and yet more at finding that I preferred it to playing duets or quiet drawing-room games.

This melancholy race round the dining-room table was repeated every Sunday evening, just at half-past ten, for two winters certainly. School was doing me no good, that was clear, and much less were impositions of any avail. All this discipline had come too late and from the wrong side; it crushed me, extinguished and stultified me. Even from the point of view of friction with other boys of my own age the object aimed at had been most effectually missed. If I had ever shared in their sports and squabbled, perhaps indeed... But I never saw them, excepting in school, under the master's rod, and that was not enough. I had grown up a too peculiar little creature to be able to catch anything of their manners, consequently I was only confirmed and strengthened in my own. They were most of them older and more forward than I was, more wide awake, too, and far more practically knowing; hence they felt a sort of hostile pity for me which I returned in scorn, well aware how incapable they would be of following me in the wide flights of my imagination.

I had never felt any pride among the peasant children of the island or of the mountains; we met on the common ground of rather primitive simplicity and extreme childishness. I had often played with them as my equals; but with these school-boys I did feel pride, and they regarded me as full of airs and affectations. It took many years to cure me of this kind of haughtiness and to come down simply to my level in the world; many years before I understood that a man is in no respect superior to his kind, because, to his sorrow, he may be a prince or a magician in the world of dreams.

LI.

THE theatre — *Peau d'Ane* — very much enlarged, with a great number of scenes, was now set up permanently in Aunt Claire's rooms. Jeanne, more interested in it since these new additions were made, came frequently; she would paint backgrounds under my instructions, and I enjoyed the moments when I could assert my authority. We had now a reserve stock-box, full of little personages, each fitted with a name and a part, and regiments of monsters, bogies and gnomes for the fairy processions, all modelled in plaster and painted in water-colour.

I remember our joy, our enthusiasm, the day when we first tried a grand semicircular back scene, which represented "Space." Little rose-colored clouds, lighted from one side, hovered in front of an expanse of blue, softened by gauze hangings, and a silken-haired fairy moved forward in the midst in a car drawn by a pair of butterflies, held up by invisible threads.

Still nothing ever came of it all because we could never set any bounds to our aspirations. Every day some new idea surged up, some more astounding scheme; and the great dress rehearsal was postponed from month to month, to some improbable future.

Every undertaking in my life will share, or has shared, the fate of the play.

LII.

OF all the masters who so cruelly ill-used me during my school life — and who all had their nicknames — by far the worst no doubt were the 'Bull-Apis' and the 'Great black Ape.' I hope that if they should happen to read this they will understand how entirely I have taken up my childish point of view to write it. If I met them now I should go up to them with hand extended and apologize for having been so refractory a pupil.

The Great Ape especially, how I hated him! When from his raised seat he would pronounce these words: "You will write out a hundred lines, you — that little milksop there," I could have flown at his face like an indignant cat. It was he who first aroused in me those bursts of sudden violence which have characterised me as a man, and which nothing foretold in the child, for I was, on the contrary, patient and gentle.

Still, it is not fair to say that I was on the whole a bad learner; unequal rather, with unexpected turns; one day at the top and at the bottom the next, but keeping up to a fair average and always at the end of the year carrying off the translation prizes. No others, that is very certain, and I only wondered that every one did not win them, the work seemed to me so easy. Compositions on the other hand I found desperately difficult, and in the form of a narrative doubly hard.

I deserted my own little room almost entirely;

it was in Aunt Claire's, under the shadow of the sugar-plum bear, that I was most resigned to the torment of lessons; on the wall, in a hidden corner of that panelled room a portrait may still be seen of the 'Great black Ape;' a sketch in pen and ink, with other fancy pictures of various worthies. The ink has faded and turned yellow, but the work of art remains intact; and when I look at it I feel once more the mortal weariness, the freezing oppression — in short the very atmosphere of school.

Aunt Claire was more than ever my friend and stand-by in these hard times, looking out the words in the dictionary and even condemning herself not unfrequently to write my impositions for the Grand Ape, in a feigned hand.

LIII.

— "BRING me, please, the second . . . No, the third drawer of my chiffonnier."

It is mamma who is speaking, amusing herself with the drawers which she has asked me to fetch every day for ever so many years, — sometimes for the pleasure of asking me to get them without really wanting them in the least. It was one of the first services that as a little child I was able to do for her; to take her one or other as the case might be, of those miniature drawers, and the tradition remained for a long time.

At the time in my life about which I am now writing, it was generally in the evening, after my return from school, that this little walk with the drawers took place, in the dusk; mamma is seated in her usual place, talking or working near the window, her work-basket before her; and the chiffonnier from the different divisions of which, she from time to time requires something, is at some little distance, in the ante-room. A chiffonnier of Louis XV. period, venerable because it belonged to our great-grandmothers. In it there were some very old little painted wooden boxes, touched no doubt every day by our ancestresses' fingers. I need hardly say that I knew all the secrets of the various divisions, kept in the same immovable order; there is a story for silks, classified in little ribbon bags; there is one for needles, one for narrow tapes, and another for little hooks. And the arrangement of these things is I doubt not the same as was made by the ancestresses whose saintly activity my mother still imitates.

To bring one of the drawers of this chiffonnier, was one of the joys, the prides of my early childhood, and nothing in their organization has changed since that day. They have ever inspired me with the tenderest respect; and are indissolubly connected in my mind with the image of my mother, and all the pretty little things, that her kind hands so dexterously made — including her last piece of embroidery which was a handkerchief for me.

Towards my seventeenth year, after terrible reverses — at a troubled period, which I shall not include in this book, but which I may as well mention, as I have already in former chapters touched upon the future — I was obliged for some months, to consider the terror of parting from my ancestral home and all the precious treasures it contained; then in the moments when I reviewed in mournful contemplation all that I valued and which was to be torn from me, one of my most bitter agonies was the thought: "I shall never again see the ante-room where the chiffonnier stands, never again carry those beloved drawers to my mother...."

And her work-basket, the very same one I begged her never to change, in spite of its being a little the worse for wear — and the various little knick-knacks it contained, cases, needle-boxes, winders and screws for her embroidery frame! — The idea that a time will come when the dear hands which make daily use of these things, will no longer do so, fills me with a dread, against which I fight in vain. Certainly as long as I live, everything will be left just as it is, and held as sacred; but after me, who will inherit this unappreciated heir-loom; what will become of these poor little trifles I love so much?

My mother's work-basket and the drawers of the chiffonnier, are what I shall leave with most grief and regret, when I am called to quit this world.

Very childish, I must confess, and I am quite ashamed of myself; — nevertheless I am almost on the verge of tears as I write it. . . .

LIV.

WITH the ever increasing worry of lessons, I had ceased for some months to read my Bible, I hardly had time in the mornings to say my prayers.

I still went to church very regularly on Sunday; indeed, we all went together. I had a great respect for the family pew, which had belonged to us for such a long time, and that place will always have a particular connection in my mind with my mother.

It was in church, however, that my faith was constantly receiving the severest shocks; those of coldness and boredom. Generally commentaries and human reasonings diminished the value of the

Bible and gospels, took away some of their grand solemn and sweet poetry. It was then very difficult to touch on such subjects to such a young mind as mine, without destroying them. It was only the family worship every evening that carried any religious conviction to me, but then the voices which read and prayed were dear to me, which made all the difference.

And then my continual contemplation of the works of nature, my meditations on the fossils of the cliffs and mountains, contained in my museum, gave birth in my innermost self to a vague unconscious pantheism.

Indeed, my faith still deeply rooted and lively as it was, was then in a state of torpor, from which at times it was capable of being roused, but which under ordinary circumstances annulled its effect. Moreover I felt a difficulty about saying my prayers; my scrupulous conscience was never easy when I knelt down — on account of my luckless tasks, always more or less shirked, and on account of my rebellions against the Bull-Apis or the Grand Ape, which I was obliged to hide, to disguise sometimes till I shuddered at the falsehood. I felt acute remorse for all this, and had periods of moral distress, to escape which I rushed more than ever into noisy games and senseless laughter, at the moment when my conscience was more particularly tender, not daring to face my parents' gaze I took refuge with the servants, and played tennis with them or skipped or romped.

For two or three years now, I had given up talking about my religious vocation; I knew now that that was at an end, had become an impossibility; but I had found nothing else to take its place. And when strangers asked what I was going to be, my parents, who were anxious about my future, did not know what to reply, still less did I. . . .

Meanwhile my brother, who also was thinking of that illegible future, one day started the idea—in one of those letters which always smelt to me of far-off, enchanted countries—that the best thing would be to make me an engineer, on account of a certain accuracy of mind, a certain facility for mathematics, which was a queer anomaly in nature like mine. And after I had been consulted, and had replied carelessly: "I am quite willing, it is all the same to me," the thing seemed decided.

This time, during which it was intended that I should go to the Polytechnic school, lasted for rather more than a year. There or elsewhere, what did it matter? When I looked at the men of a certain age who surrounded me, even those who occupied the most honourable positions, the most justly respected, whom I could hope to imitate, and said to myself: "One day I shall be like them, live a useful steady life *in a given place, in a determined sphere*, and then grow old, that is all"—I was seized with a nameless despair; I wished for nothing that was either possible or reasonable; I longed more than ever to remain always a child, and the thought that years were fleeting, and that in spite of everything I must soon be a man, was unspeakably agonizing.

LV.

TWICE a week, in the history class, I was thrown together with the naval students, who wore red belts to give themselves a sailor-like air, and who drew anchors and boats in their school-books.

I had never thought of the sea as my own calling; once or twice at most the idea had crossed my mind but with a sense of uneasiness. And yet it was the only profession which could have the attraction of voyages and adventure; only it alarmed me more than any other on account of the long periods of exile which my faith would no longer help me to endure, as in the days when I had meant to be a missionary.

To go away like my brother; to leave my mother and all I loved for years; never, for years to see my dear little garden grow green in the spring, and the roses blossom on the old walls;— no, I had not courage enough for that.

All the more because it seemed to me, no doubt as a result of my peculiar education, a foregone conclusion that so rough a life could never be mine. And I knew too, from words that had been spoken in my hearing, that if ever such a wild idea should come into my head my parents would utterly refuse, never, on any terms consent.

LVI.

VERY home-sick now were the feelings I found in my museum when I went up there in the winter half-holidays after finishing my tasks and 'impositions'—always rather late. The light was fading by that time, and the glimpse I got of the distant level was veiled by a rosy gray haze, sad beyond words. My home-sickness was for the summer, for the sun and the South; and it was brought on by the sight of all the butterflies from my uncle's garden pinned in rows under glass, and of all the mountain fossils, picked up out there with the little Peyrals. This was a foretaste of those regrets for 'somewhere'—anywhere—which in later years after my long voyages in the tropics, spoiled my return home in the winter season.

And above all the orange-sulphur butterfly! There were times when I found a bitter joy in gazing at it, in dwelling on the melancholy it roused in me, and trying to understand it. It was in one of the back cases; its too 'bright and strangely contrasted hues, like those of a Chinese painting or a fairy's robe, each heightened by the other, seemed almost luminous when grey twilight fell, and the other butterflies near it looked no better than dingy little bats.

As soon as my eye fell on it, I could hear the drawling, sleepy tune in the peculiar mountain-treble: "*Ah, ah, la bonne histoire!*" and I could see the white porch of the house at Bories, in the sunlit silence of summer noons. A dreadful regret would come over me for those past holidays; I sadly counted back the long days since they were past, and the longer time to the holidays to come; and then other feelings for which there were no words would crowd in, rising up from the unsounded inner depths and mingling in a strange whole.

This association of the butterfly, the song, and Bories, for a long time caused me fits of melancholy which nothing that I can write will ever express; and this went on till the great storm swept over my life carrying away most of these memories of my childhood.

Sometimes in the calm grey winter evenings, as I looked at the butterfly, I would go so far as to sing the plaintive little air, in the flute-like pipe proper to it; and then the house at Bories rose up before my eyes even more distinctly, sunny but deserted in a September morning; it was something of the same kind which afterwards impressed on me the association of the wailing treble of Arab songs with the whiteness of their mosques — the winding-sheets of whitewash in which they wrap their gateways.

That butterfly is still there, in all the sheen of its two singular hues, mummified in its glass-case, just as bright as ever. It is to me a sort of fetich to which I am greatly attached. The little Sainte-Hermangardes, — of whom I lost sight many years ago and who are now attachés to some Eastern embassy — will be greatly surprised, if they should read this, to learn how precious circumstances have made their gift.

LVII.

THE great event of these winters, prisoned as they were now by school-life, was the festival of New Year's gifts. By the end of November we three —my sister, Lucette and I — were in the habit of publishing a list of the things we wished for. Everybody in the two families prepared surprises for us, and the mystery in which those presents were wrapped was my chief amusement during the last days of the year. My parents, grandmother and aunts delighted in exciting my curiosity by constant hints among themselves, and whisperings which they affected to break off as soon as I came into the room.

Between Lucette and me it became quite a game of guessing As in playing, "How, when and where," there were certain questions we allowed each other — for instance so absurd an inquiry as: "Has it hairs like a beast?" And the answers would be something to this effect: "The thing your father is going to give you had hairs but has lost them (a leather dressing-case), but it has false hair on part of its inside (the brushes). What your mamma will give you has some still (a muff). What your aunt will give you will help you see them, but I don't think — stay — no, I don't *think* it has any of its own (a lamp).

Through the dusk hours of December, as we sat on low stools, in front of the blazing oak logs, this was the catechism we carried on, more eagerly every day till the 31st, the great evening of unveiled mysteries.

That evening all the presents from and for both families were addressed and placed on the tables in a room which Lucette and I were forbidden to enter all day. At eight o'clock the door was opened and every one admitted in a crowd, the grandparents first, each one seeking his own in the pile of paper parcels tied up with ribbon. To me the joy of that moment was such that even when I was twelve or thirteen I could not refrain from cutting capers at the door before I was let in.

At eleven o'clock we had supper; and then, when the dining-room clock, with its calm unmoved tinkle, struck twelve, we went to bed, during those first minutes of the far away years buried under the dust of so many successors.

I went to sleep with all my treasures in my room, with the most precious of them on the bed. And I woke earlier than usual next morning to look at them; they cast an enchantment over the winter's dawn, the first of a new year.

Once, there was among the number a large book full of prints, and treating of the antediluvian world. Fossils had already initiated me into the mystery of wrecked creations. I knew several of the ponderous beasts which in geological eras had shaken the primeval forests with their heavy tread; I had been thinking about them for a long time — and here I found them all in their habitat, under the leaden sky, among the tall tree-ferns.

The antediluvian world, which already floated in my imagination, became the frequent theme of my imaginings; I often tried by concentrating my fancy, to call up a picture of some monstrous landscape, in the same gloomy twilight with dark distances; then, when the image thus evoked had become as real as a vision, it gave rise to an extreme and nameless dejection, as if it were breathing forth its soul — and that was the end — it vanished.

It was not long before I had sketched a new scene for *Pean d'Ane*, representing a landscape of the Lias: a dismal swamp in a half-light shrouded by banks of clouds, where the beasts of the past prowled among tree-ferns and mares'-tails. But indeed *Peau d'Ane* had by this time lost its identity. I had by degrees given up the actors whose intolerable fixity as dolls had ceased to interest me; they were sleeping already, poor little things, in their boxes from which no doubt they will never be exhumed. My new scenes had nothing whatever to do with the piece; they were glades in virgin-forests, exotic gardens, oriental palaces of gold and mother-of-pearl — all my dreams, in short, which I strove to realize with the small means at my command while waiting for better, the improbable " better " of the future.

LVIII.

MEANWHILE, after this wretched winter spent under the auspices of the "Bull-Apis" and the Grand-Ape, the spring returned, a fever in the blood of school-boys who long to be out and about, who can scarcely sit still and who are beside themselves at the first warm days. The roses were budding all over our old walls; my dear little garden was as tempting as ever in the March sunshine, and I lingered late there watching the insects awake and the first butterflies and bees take wing. Even my theatre was forgotten.

I was no longer taken to school and fetched away; I had succeeded in abrogating that custom which made me ridiculous in the eyes of my companions. And on my way home I would often make a little round by the quiet ramparts, whence I could see the villages beyond and a glimpse of the country in the distance. But I worked more carelessly than ever that spring; the lovely weather turned my brain.

One of the exercises in which I most ignominiously failed was certainly French composition; I had nothing to show but the bare canvas without the faintest attempt at embroidery. There was one boy in the class who was a master in this style and whose great works were always read aloud. Oh what beautiful things he could find to stuff in, to be sure! — He became the most prosaic of officials in a little manufacturing town. One day, the theme being, "A Shipwreck," he had hit on a lyric flow! — while I had given in a blank sheet with the title and my name signed. I could not make up my mind to elaborate the subjects set us by the Great-Ape; a sort of instinctive decency kept me from fluent commonplace, and as to writing what I really felt, the notion of its being read and mangled by that ogre stopped that entirely.

Still, I was even then fond of writing, for myself alone and under a shroud of inviolable mystery. Not in the desk in my room which was desecrated by my school-books and exercises, but in the little old desk which formed part of the furniture of my museum there was a quaint document which stood for a diary in my first manner. It looked like some fairy manuscript or Assyrian roll. An endless strip of paper was rolled round a reed; at the beginning were two Egyptian-looking sphinxes in red ink, and a cabalistic star; and then it began, written in a cryptogram of my own invention. It was not till a year after this that I adopted ordinary writing because the elaborate cypher took so long, but I still kept it hidden, locked up as if it were a crime. In this, beyond the events of my very uneventful life, I only noted my incoherent impressions, my evening melancholy, my grieving over past summers and dreams of distant lands. I already felt that craving to make such notes, to fix these fugitive images, to struggle against the evanescence of things and of myself, which has made me keep my journal regularly down to these later years. But at that time the mere idea that any one should ever set eyes on it was intolerable to me; to such a point that whenever I went any little journey—to the island, or elsewhere—I always took care to seal it up and write solemnly on the wrapper: "It is my last desire that this book should be burnt unread."

Dear Heaven! I have changed since then.— But it would be quite outside the limits of this story of my childhood to give any account here of the chances and changes which have led me rather to proclaim my woe and declare it to those who pass by, to attract the sympathy of the unknown and remote; — aye, and to cry all the

home unchanged; those years of exile really had an end; they already began to seem shorter than I had formerly thought them. My brother, too, would return next autumn. We should soon feel as if we had never parted.

And what a joy such a return must be! What a glory seemed to shroud those who had come from so far.

Next day, in Jeanne's garden, I saw enormous foreign cases being unpacked; some were wrapped in tarpaulin, pieces of old sails no doubt, full of the fresh fragrance of ships and the sea; two sailors in their blue collars were busy uncording and unscrewing them, and they took out of them mysterious-looking objects which smelt of "the colonies:" mats, and water jars, and vases; even some coconuts and other foreign fruits. Jeanne's grandfather, himself an old sailor, was standing by me watching the unpacking out of the corner of his eye, when suddenly from between the boards of a case which they were breaking open, we saw some horrid brown beetles crawl out in a great hurry; whereupon the sailors jumped upon them with both feet to kill them.

"Cockroaches, eh, captain?" I asked of the grandfather.

"So you know them do you, little landlubber?" said he, laughing.

To tell the truth I had never seen one, but uncles of mine who had lived in their society had told me about them. And I was delighted at my first introduction to these creatures which belong so essentially to hot countries and shipboard.

LX.

SPRING! Spring! On the garden walls the white roses were in bloom, the jasmine, the honeysuckles, hanging in long garlands of delicious fragrance.

I lived there again now from morning till night; lived there with the plants and the old stones, listening to the plash of water under the great plum-tree, examining the grasses and woodland mosses which had lost their way and established themselves on the edge of my pool, or on the opposite side where the sun shone, counting the buds on the cactus. My Wednesday evening journeys to *la Limoise* had begun again too, and I dreamed of nothing else, I need hardly say, from week's end to week's end, to the great neglect of my lessons and exercises.

LXI.

I REALLY believe that the spring of that year was the most brilliant, the most heady of all the springs of my childhood; in contrast no doubt with the miserable winter over which the Grand-Ape had loomed a tyrant. Ah! the last days of May with the deep grass, and the mowing and hay-making of June! In what a golden glory I see it all again.

My evening walks with my father and sister

continued throughout the early years of my life; they used to come and wait for me at half-past four, when I came out of school, and we set off at once for the fields. Our particular fancy that year was for certain meadows full of pink campion, and I always brought home sheaves of these flowers. In the same meadows an ephemeral race of little pink and black butterflies had come to life, and the same pink as the campion, which rested on the tall stems, and fluttered away like flower-petals blown-off, as we stirred the hay grass. I see it all again in the exquisitely limpid atmosphere of June. At afternoon class the thought of the wide fields waiting for me out there, disturbed me even more than the soft breeze and spring odours which came in at the open windows.

I remember best of all one evening when my mother had promised that she too, for a great treat, would come for a walk to see the fields of pink campion. On that occasion, having been more inattentive than usual, the Grand-Ape had threatened to keep me in, and all through the lesson I fancied I was going to be punished. This keeping in of an evening, which detained us in school for an hour longer in the delicious June weather, was always a cruel torment. But that day especially my heart was full, at thinking that mamma would be waiting for me and that the springs were so short, and that the hay would soon be cut, and that such another lovely evening might not shine on us this year.

Lessons being over I anxiously examined the fateful list in the monitor's hand. My name was not on it! The Grand-Ape had forgotten me or been merciful.

Oh! my joy, as I ran out of school, at finding mamma who had kept her word, and who was waiting for me smiling, with my father and sister. The air outside was more delicious than ever, warm and odorous, and the light had a tropical glory. When I recall that time, those fields of wild flowers, those pink butterflies, a sort of indefinable anxiety mingles with my fond regret, as it always does when I conjure up the things which have struck and enchanted me by some mysterious nether current, and I cannot account for its intensity.

LXII.

AS I have said, I was always very young of my age. If I could be set face to face, just as I was then, with some of the youth of Paris, of thirteen and fourteen, brought up on the most improved and modern methods, who can already recite and speechify, and have notions on politics, and petrify me by their conversations, how funny it would be and how they would scorn me.

Indeed, I myself am surprised at the amount of childishness which still clung to me in certain points; for, in spite of a lack of method and of acquirements, in matters of art and fancy I went further and soared higher than I do now, there is no question; and if that scrawl rolled on a reed of which I spoke just now, were still in existence it would have twenty times the value of these pale reminiscences, on which, as it seems to me, ashes are already strewn.

LXIII.

MY room, into which I never went now to do my tasks, rarely, indeed, excepting at night to sleep, became to me a scene of delight again during the long warm twilights of this lovely June, after dinner was over. I had invented a game for myself, a sort of improved tip-cat, and this amused me in an extraordinary degree; I was never tired of it. It would amuse me just as much to this day if I dared do it, and I can only hope that my game may find imitators among all the children who are imprudently permitted to read this chapter.

Thus it was: just opposite me and on the first floor, dwelt a good old maid known as Mademoiselle Victoire, with great old-fashioned cap-borders and large round spectacles. I had obtained her permission to fix a line of pack-thread to the peg that fastened back her shutter, and the other end was wound round a stick in my room on the other side of the street.

In the evening, as it grew dusk, a bird of my own construction — a sort of blundering crow made of wire with black silk wings — stole out from between my shutters, which I immediately closed again, and fell struggling and flopping on the pavement, in the middle of the street. The ring to which it was attached slid on the string which in the dusk was invisible, and I kept it hopping and jumping on the ground flapping very comically. Then when a passerby stooped to see what this queer creature was that jumped so incessantly, crack! I twitched the string very hard, and the bird flew up into the air hitting him on the nose.

Oh! Did not I have fun those fine summer twilights lurking behind my shutters; did not I laugh all alone, at the shrieks and alarms and conjectures to which they gave rise. What amazes me is that after the first fright every one laughed as heartily as I did; most of them, to be sure, were neighbours, who might guess at the author of this practical joke, and I was a favourite in the quarter in those days. Or else they were sailors, good-natured souls, generally very indulgent to childish tricks—and with good reason.

But the thing which will always remain inexplicable is that my family, who as a rule sinned on the side of preciseness, could shut their eyes to this sport, and indeed tacitly allow it through one whole spring. I have never been able to account for this want of propriety; and years, instead of clearing up this mystery, have only made it seem more astounding.

The black bird is, I need hardly say, preserved as one of my many relics; now and then every two or three years I get it out to look at—a little mite-eaten, but reminding me still of the lovely evenings of departed Junes and the delicious intoxication of my childhood's springs.

LXIV.

ON those Thursdays at *la Limoise*, in the torrid sunshine, when all nature slept exhausted in the silent country, I had made it a habit to climb up the wall at the bottom of the garden and sit perched there, astride, without stirring from the spot, buried up to my ears in ivy, with the grasshoppers and flies buzzing all round me. I looked out over the deserted, baking landscape as from an observatory—the heath, the woods, and the filmy haze of mirage which the heat kept in a constant tremulous ripple like the surface of a lake. The distant views still had for me that mystery of the unknown which I had lent them in the earlier summers of my life. I pictured to myself that the rather desolate tract I could see from this dale stretched away indefinitely in heath and forest, like a really primitive country; and though I knew now that not far away there were roads and farms, and towns, as there were everywhere else, it did not matter; I could still delude myself as to the wildness of these distances.

Indeed, to cheat myself, I took care to hold up my hand like a spy-glass, so as to shut out everything which could spoil the desert view; an old farmhouse, for instance, a patch of vineyard, and a glimpse of the wood. So up there, all alone, with nothing to disturb the silence but the hum of insects, by always looking through my hand only in the direction where there was least cultivation, I managed to give myself a very sufficient sense of a wild and foreign land.

More especially of Brazil. Why Brazil I know not; but it was Brazil which the neighbouring wood represented to my fancy in these hours of contemplation.

I must pause for a moment to describe this wood, the first wood on earth that I ever loved; very old evergreen oaks, never stripped of their deep green leaves, formed a sort of colonnade like a temple of noble trunks; and beneath their shade not a shrub, but a quite peculiar character of soil, always dry, covered all the year round with exquisitely fine grass, as close and minute as a growth of down, with here and there a few ferns and a very few shade-loving flowers.

LXV.

THE Iliad was the lesson we were studying in class, and I might have loved it no doubt, but that it had been made odious to me with parsing, and 'impositions' and parrot-like repetition; and suddenly I paused, moved to admiration by the famous line:

Βῆ δ'ἀκέων παρὰ θῖνα πολυφλοίσβοιο θαλάσσης

which ends like the splash of a wave at high tide as it spreads its foam on a pebbly beach.

"Observe," says the Grand-Ape, "observe the imitative harmony."

Oh yes, never fear; I had observed it. No need to bid me observe anything of that kind.

A CHILD'S ROMANCE.

One of the things I most admired, with less justice perhaps, was this passage of Virgil:

Hinc adeo media est nobis via; namque sepulcrum Incipit apparere Bianoris :...

From the very beginning of the eclogue I had watched the two shepherds making their way across the antique landscape. I could see it plainly: the Roman campagna two thousand years ago; hot, rather bare, with clumps of butcher's broom and evergreen oak, like the stony district of *la Limoise*, in which I found the same old world pastoral charm.

On they went, those two shepherds, and presently perceived that they were half-way, because the sepulchre of Bianoris was in sight. I could see that too, that tomb. Its old stones stood out, a white spot on the reddish road covered with low-growing herbs, rather burnt up, wild thyme or marjoram, and here and there a hungry, dark-leaved shrub. The sonorous name *Bianoris*, ending the phrase, suddenly gave me with magical vividness the impression of the music made by the insects as they buzzed round the travellers in the stillness of a very hot noon, lighted up by a younger sun under the serene quiet of an ancient month of June. I was no longer in school; I was out on the campagna in the company of those two shepherds, walking on the scorched wild flowers and sunburnt grass, under a very brilliant summer sky—but yet all thin and faint, seen vaguely, as it were through a telescope, in the remote past.

Who knows! If the Grand-Ape could have guessed whither my mind had wandered, it might perhaps have drawn us together a little.

LXVI.

ON a certain Thursday evening, at *la Limoise*, while awaiting the inevitable moment of departure, I had gone upstairs alone to the great old bedroom on the first floor, which was mine. At first I stood with my elbows on the window-sill to watch the July sun sink crimson behind the stony plain and the ferny moor towards the sea beyond, which though not distant was invisible. So melancholy, always, were these sunsets at the end of my Thursday holiday.

And then, at the last moment, just before starting, I took it into my head, as I had never done before, to rummage in the old Louis XV. book-case by the side of my bed. There, among the books in their last century bindings, where maggots, undisturbed, were diligently eating out their galleries, I found a note-book covered with rare old-fashioned paper, and I opened it without thought. And there I learnt with a thrill of excitement that "from noon till four o'clock on the 20th of June, 1813, in long. 110 E. and lat. 15 S. (thus between the tropics and in the wide Pacific) the weather was fine, sea smooth, a light breeze from the southwest, the sky covered with the light clouds known as mares'-tails, and many flying-fish alongside."

Dead, long ago, were the eyes which had observed the fugitive cloud-shapes, and watched the flying-fish. The note-book, as I at once perceived, was one of those records known as log-books, kept day by day on board ship; it did not astonish me as a novelty, though I had never before had one in my hands. Still, it was a strange and unexpected thing to find myself thus suddenly initiated into the familiar aspects of sky and ocean on the high Pacific seas, on a particular day now so long ago. Oh! To see them with my own eyes! The smooth, calm sea, the mares'-tails streaking the deep immensity of the blue sky, and the swift flying-fish cleaving the tropical solitude.

What delightful things there must be in that sailor-life which terrified me and was prohibited to me! I had never felt it so keenly as this evening. The ineffaceable memory of this stolen reading was the cause of my never failing to look over the ship's side if a shoal of flying-fish was reported by the steersman when I happened to be on watch; and I have always felt distinct pleasure in recording the incident in the log-book so like that kept by the seamen of 1813 before me.

LXVII.

IN the following holidays our departure for the South and the mountains was a greater joy than it had been the first time. As in the previous year, my sister and I set out at the beginning of August; no longer on a voyage of discovery, it is true; but the delight of going back again and finding everything there which had charmed me so much, was even greater than that of the journey into the unknown.

Between the place where the railway ended and the little town where the cousins lived, a long drive in a hired carriage, our little coachman took us by cross-country cuts, lost his way, and carried us we knew not where, but into the most delicious nooks of country. The weather was splendid, wonderful. How gleefully I hailed the first peasant-women carrying large copper water-jars on their heads, the first tanned labourers talking *patois*, the first fields of red earth and the first mountain junipers.

In the middle of day, during a halt to rest the horses in the hollow of a shady dell, by a remote village called Veyrac, we sat down under a chestnut tree, and we were there besieged by the ducks of the place, the most audacious and ill-bred ducks in the world, which gathered round us in force with the most outrageous quacking. When we were setting off again in the carriage, with the absurd creatures still in pursuit, my sister turned to them, and said with the dignity of the traveller of antiquity who was insulted by an inhospitable populace: "Ducks of Veyrac, be ye accursed!"—After all these years I cannot think calmly of the fit of laughing this gave rise to. And above all I can never remember the day without a regret for that glory of sunshine and blue sky, such I have no eyes to see now.

On our arrival we found a party waiting for us by the roadside, at the bridge over the river—our cousins and the little Peyrals, waving their handkerchiefs.

I was happy at meeting my little band all complete. We had all grown a little and were taller by an inch or so; but we saw at once that this had made no difference, that we were as much as ever children, and inclined for the same games.

At dusk there was a tremendous storm; and while it was thundering as if a whole battery of artillery were being discharged on my uncle's roof, while from all the old gargoyles in the village torrents of water were rushing down the black pebbles of the street pavement, the little Peyrals and I took refuge in the kitchen, to make a noise and dance at our ease.

A very large kitchen; furnished in the old fashion, with an arsenal of copper pots and pans, kettles and frying-pans, hung against the wall in order of size and glittering like plate armour. It was almost dark; the good smell of the storm was rising up — of wet earth and summer rain, and through the deep iron-barred Louis XIII. windows the broad green flashes came in every minute, blinding us and compelling us to shut our eyes in spite of ourselves.

We spun and spun like crazy things singing a sentimental tune which, as it had certainly never been composed to be danced to, we scanned with absurd false emphasis to make it suit our round-about whirl. How long this gleeful saraband may have lasted I do not know; the storm had excited us to frenzy, and the wild noise we made and our vehement tee-totum went to our brain, like little dervishes; it was all in honour of my return and a way of worthily beginning the holidays; of laughing at the Grand-Ape, and inaugurating the endless excursions and childish games of every kind which began again more than ever on the morrow.

LXVIII.

NEXT morning I awoke at daybreak, hearing a regular clatter which I had lost the habit of being used to; the weaver close by, beginning already at dawn the to and fro of the hereditary shuttle. Then, upon a single moment of indecision, I remembered with exuberant joy that I had just come to the South; that it was the morning of the first day; that a whole summer of open air and free device lay before me: August and September, two months such as now fly like a single day, but then seemed very respectably long. It was with real rapture that I awoke to consciousness after a good night's sleep. "I had joy in waking."

I had remembered from some book I had read during the past winter, some story of the North American Lake Indians, an incident which had struck my fancy: An old Red-skin, whose daughter was pining for love of a Pale-face, had at last consented to give her to the stranger, " to the end that she might once more have joy in waking."

Joy in waking! Yes, for some time I had learned to note that the moment of waking is always that in which we have the most vivid impression of what ever is bright or sad in life, and find it most acutely painful to lack joy; my first little sorrows, my first little remorse, my terrors for the future, were always most urgent at that moment of the day — to vanish forthwith, it is true at that age.

My waking moments were to be gloomier as time went on, and they are now instants of terrific lucidity when I see the under side — the seamy side of life, stripped of the mirages which during the day still divert my mind and still veil it; when I most clearly see the swift flight of years, the crumbling of everything to which I try to cling, and the final void, the gaping gulf of death, close at hand and bare of all disguise.

But that morning I had joy in waking. And I got up early, not being able to rest content in my bed, eager to be out and about, and wondering where I should begin my round of visits and inspection.

There were all the old corners of the town to be seen, and the gothic ramparts, and the delicious river. — And my uncle's garden, where, since last year, the most impossible butterflies might perhaps have chosen to settle. And visits to pay in strange old houses, to all the good women of the neighbourhood, who last year had loaded me with all the best grapes off their vines as though it were tribute due to me; one Madame Jeanne, more especially, a rich old peasant woman who had quite an adoration for me and fulfilled all my behests, and who, whenever she passed homewards, like Nausicaa from the washing place, shot side-long glances at my uncle's house, for my particular benefit, which were comical beyond words. — And then the vineyards and woods outside and the mountain paths, and Castelnau out there, lifting its battlemented towers above the pedestal of chesnuts and oaks, and inviting me to its ruins. Where should I go first, and how be ever weary of such a land!

The sea, whither indeed I was rarely taken now, I had for the time completely forgotten.

After two months of happiness the dreadful return to lessons, which I could not help thinking of, was to be relieved by my brother's first homecoming. His four years of absence were not quite yet ended, but we knew that he had left the mysterious island and was to be expected in October. To me it would be a new acquaintance to make; I wondered uneasily whether he would love me when he saw me, whether he would like me, whether a thousand details — for instance, my way of playing Beethoven — would be to his taste.

I thought incessantly of his arrival, now so near; I was so delighted at the prospect and looked forward to such a complete change in my life that I quite forgot my usual autumn terrors.

But I intended to ask his advice too about a thousand things that troubled me, and confide to him all my anxieties as to the future. I knew, indeed, that his opinion was to be taken as to some definite plan for me, to direct my studies and decide on my career; that was the black spot on his return.

Pending this momentous fiat I would find as much amusement and forgetfulness as possible without any cares for the morrow, giving myself every enjoyment, and more than ever, during these holidays, which I regarded as the last of my child-life.

LXIX.

AFTER our mid-day dinner it was the custom of the house to sit for an hour or two in the stone-floored entrance hall, with its great red copper cistern; it was the coolest spot during the oppressive heat of the day. It was kept dark by closing every door and shutter; only two or three shafts of sunshine in which the flies sported, streamed in through the cracks of the heavy Louis XIII. front door. But in the silent village, where no one was stirring, there was nothing to be heard but the eternal chatter of hens; every other creature seemed to be asleep.

I did not stay in the cool hall, not I. The blazing sun outside tempted me; and besides, no sooner had we settled down than we heard tap-tap at the front door; the Peyrals, come to fetch me, and all three lifting and dropping the old iron knocker, so hot that it made their fingers tingle.

Then, with our hats well over our eyes, away

we went on some fresh enterprise every day, with hammers, sticks and butterfly nets. First along the narrow cobble-stoned streets; then by the first paths outside the village, which were always deep in a bed of chaff, in which we sank up to our ancles and which filled our shoes; then, at last, came the open country, the vineyards and paths up the hillside — or the river, which we could cross on stepping-stones, with its islands full of flowers.

As a contrast to my coddled and too quiet life at home nothing could be more complete; but still I lacked the company of other boys of my own age and wholesome friction; besides it only lasted two months.

LXX.

ONE day, out of impudence, in sheer bravado — I know not really why, I took into my head that I should like to do something thoroughly nasty. And after having thought of what it should be all one morning I hit upon it.

Everyone knows the swarms of flies which we have in the summer in the Southern provinces, fouling everything, a perfect scourge. In the middle of my uncle's kitchen a trap was laid for them, a sort of treacherous drinking place of a particular shape where, at the bottom they were inevitably drowned in soapy water. Well, that day I discerned at the bottom of this jar a horrible black mass formed of the myriads of flies which had been drowned there these two or three days, and it struck me that I might have them made into a dish — a pancake or an omelette.

Very hurriedly, with a feeling of disgust amounting to nausea, I turned the black mess into a plate and carried it off privily to old Madame Jeanne, my faithful adorer, the only person in the world who would do anything and everything for me.

"An *omelette aux mouches!* Why, to be sure, what would be simpler?" said she. Fire, frying-pan, eggs at once, and the filthy thing, well beaten, was set to cook in the great mediæval hearth while I looked on horrified and disgusted with myself.

Then came the three little Peyrals, and comforted me by going into ecstasies over my idea — as they always did, and when the dish was done to a turn and served up all hot, we went off in triumph to show it to our elders, marching in procession and singing in our deepest bass voices, as if we were carrying the devil to the grave.

LXXI.

THE end of the summer was especially delicious out there, when the meadows were purple with autumn crocus in front of the yellowing woods. Then the vintage began, lasting at least a fortnight and perfectly enchanting us. In the little glades of the woods, or the fields adjoining the Peyrals' vineyards, where we spent all our days; we made feasts of bonbons and fruit, laying the fruit out on the grass in the most elegant manner, surrounded in the antique style with garlands, and with large yellow or red vine leaves to serve as plates. The vintagers would bring us the most exquisite grapes, chosen out of thousands of bunches; with the help of the sun we were sometimes really a little tipsy, not with sweet wine even, for we had none, but simply with grapes, as the wasps and bees get tipsy in the sun on a vine-trellice.

One morning at the end of September, when the weather was rainy and chill and had a melancholy flavour of autumn, I went into the kitchen, attracted by a fire of brushwood which was blazing merrily in the high old chimney. And being there, idle and put out by the rain, to amuse myself I melted an old pewter plate, and let it drop, all hot and liquid, into a pail of water. It took the shape of an irregular, distorted mass of a fine silvery white and looking something like ore. I gazed at it thoughtfully for a long time: an idea was forming in my mind, a scheme for a new form of amusement which might perhaps be the crowning delight of the remaining days of the holidays. That very evening in a committee held on the steps of the great staircase, with its forged iron railings, I explained to the little Peyrals that I had an idea, from the appearance of the soil and the plants, that perhaps there might be silver mines in this part of the country. And I gave myself such a lofty buccaneering air as stamps the leading figures in the old-fashioned novels of which the scene is laid in America.

To seek for mines was quite in the spirit of my little band, who were used to setting out with spades and picks to seek for fossils or rare pebbles.

So on the following day, half way up the mountain side, as we came to a delightful path, very lonely and mysterious, overhung with trees, and deep between two high moss-grown banks, I stopped the party with the dignity of a Red-skin scout. It would be here; I had detected the presence of deposits of treasure — and sure enough, by digging on the spot I pointed out, we found the first nuggets: the melted plate which I had come to bury there the day before.

These mines were our one idea till the end of the season. They were perfectly convinced and amazed; and even I, who melted down pewter plates and covers every morning to keep up the supply of silver ore, almost persuaded myself to believe in them. The lonely spot, exquisite and still, where the diggings were, and the serene pathos of the dying summer threw a rare charm over our dream of adventure. We kept our discoveries a deep and amusing mystery, as a sort of tribal secret among ourselves. And our riches, mixed with a little red earth of the mountain, were stored in an old trunk in my uncle's loft, as in Ali Baba's cave. We determined to leave them there all the winter, till next year's holidays, and then we would add greatly to our treasure.

LXXII.

AT the beginning of October we were recalled home by a glad telegram from my father. My brother, who had returned to Europe by a mail packet from Panama, had disembarked at Southampton; we had only just time to hurry home if we wished to be there to welcome him.

On the evening of the next day but one we arrived in the very nick of time, for he was to be expected a few hours later by a night train. There was only time to replace in his room, where they had formerly stood, the different little ornaments he had entrusted to my care four years since, before we had to start to meet him at the station. To me it seemed all unreal. I could not believe in this return, especially at such sudden notice, and I had not slept for two nights past. I was dropping with sleep as we waited at the station, in spite of my extreme impatience, and it was as in a dream that I saw him, and embraced him, feeling shy at finding him so unlike the remembrance I had preserved of him; sunburnt, with his beard much thicker, his words fewer, and eyes that scrutinized me with a half-smiling, half-anxious expression, as if to detect what the years were beginning to make of me and what I might turn out by and bye.

As we went home I fairly fell asleep as I stood, overcome by a child's heaviness when worn out by a long journey, quite impossible to fight against, and I was sent to bed.

LXXIII.

WAKING next morning with a sudden consciousness of something happy in the air and a sense of joy at the bottom of my soul, I at once saw an object of extraordinary outline, on a table in my room; evidently a canoe from the antipodes, very long and strange-looking with its outrigger and sails. Then my eyes fell on more unknown objects; necklaces of shells threaded on human hair, feather head-dresses, ornaments of gloomy and primitive savage simplicity, hung about in every direction as if distant Polynesia had come to me during the night. — So my brother had begun to unpack his cases, and he must have crept in quietly while I was still asleep and amused himself with arranging these presents intended for my museum.

I jumped up and dressed quickly to go and find him, for I had hardly seen him the night before.

LXXIV.

AND indeed I hardly saw him during the few hurried weeks he spent at home with us. Of that time, so short as it was, I have none but confused memories such as remain of the objects seen as we fly past them on horseback. I vaguely recollect that his presence brought a gayer and younger bustle of existence into the house. I remember, too, that at times he seemed to be absorbed in thought over matters altogether outside our family circle; regrets perhaps for the hot countries, and the "delicious island," or anxieties as to his too near departure.

Sometimes I could keep him a captive to the piano with Chopin's hallucinating music, which was to me then a new discovery. He was a little uneasy about its effect; it was too much for me, he said, too enervating. Having just come into our midst he was better able to form an opinion, and he perceived no doubt that I was really being over-forced on the artistic side, it must be understood; that Chopin and *Peau d'Ane* were equally bad for me; that I was acquiring an overwrought refinement in spite of my incoherent fits of childishness, and that almost all my amusements were of the order of dreams. So one day, to my great delight, he decreed that I must learn to ride; but this was the only great change in my education which his visit made. As to the serious questions concerning the future which I so much wanted to discuss with him, I constantly put them off, fearing to approach such subjects and preferring to gain time, to postpone the decision and so, as it were, to prolong my childhood. And after all there was no hurry; he was to be with us for years.

And one fine morning — when we were so sure of keeping him — from the admirality, there came for him, with a new grade, the order to set out without delay for the furthest East where an expedition was being fitted out.

So after a few days more which were spent in preparations for this unlooked-for naval campaign, he was gone, as though swept away by a gust of wind.

Our leave-takings were, however, less sad on this occasion because, as we believed, his absence would not extend over two years. And in fact he was gone forever; his body was to be thrown overboard somewhere in the heart of the Indian ocean, about the middle of the Gulf of Bengal.

When he was gone, while we could still hear the sound of the carriage wheels, my mother turned to me with a look in her eyes which at once moved the inmost fibres of my heart, and then, drawing me to her she said in a tone of perfect confidence: "Thank God, we shall keep you, at any rate!"

Keep me! — me! Oh! — I hung my head, averting my eyes which must have changed their expression and become a little wild perhaps. I could not find a word or a caress in response to my mother. This serene confidence was a pang, to me, for the mere fact of hearing her say " We shall keep you," made me understand for the first time in my life how far the hardly conscious purpose of going away, too, had already progressed in my mind; of going even farther than my brother; of going everywhere, all over the world.

The notion of the navy still frightened me, nevertheless; I did not love it, oh no! Only to think of it made my heart ache, home-loving little creature that I was, too closely bound by a thousand soft ties. Besides, how could I ever confess the thought to my parents, how could I pain them so much, or rebel so greatly?— Still, to give it all up, to stay all my life in one spot, to part from earth without ever having seen it— what a disenchanting prospect! What was the use of living, of growing up, then?

And there, in the empty drawing-room where the displaced furniture and a chair overturned were full of the sad hurry of parting, as I stood close to my mother, my eyes fixed on vacancy and my soul in a tumult, I suddenly remembered the log-book of those bygone mariners, which I had read by the light of the setting sun that spring at *la Limoise*; the short sentences written in tawny ink on old paper slowly came back to me, one after another, with a treacherous and soothing charm, like what I can fancy a magic incantation.

"Weather fine; sea smooth; a light breeze from the southeast; shoals of flying-fish to starboard."

It was with a thrill of almost religious awe, a sort of pantheistic rapture that the vision rose around me of the South Pacific ocean, solemn and infinite and dazzling blue.

LXXV.

A MELANCHOLY calm succeeded my brother's departure, and the days followed each other in absolute monotony.

I was probably to be sent to the *École Poly-*

technique, though this was not finally determined on. The idea of being a sailor, which had grown up in me in spite of myself, bewitched and terrified me in an almost equal degree. For lack of courage to open up so serious a question I always shrank from mentioning it; I even concluded that I would still think the matter over till the next holidays, allowing myself these few months as a last reprieve to my childish irresolution and carelessness.

I lived just as much alone as ever; my taste for solitude was by this time confirmed and difficult to break through, in spite of my anxieties and my latent passion for freedom and running about the world. I spent most of my time at home, busy painting strange scenery, or playing Chopin and Beethoven, content, to all seeming, and absorbed in dreams; and every day I grew fonder of my home, of its every nook and corner, and the very stones of its walls. I rode on horseback now, it is true, but always with a servant, never with any one of my own age. I still had no playfellows.

However, my second year of school-life

seemed less dreadful than the first; it passed less slowly, and I had at last made friends with two bigger boys, my seniors by a year or two; the only lads who, the year before, had not treated me as an impracticable little being. The ice once broken we three at once became fast friends of the most sentimental type; we even called each other by our Christian names, quite against the common law of manners in schools. And as we never by any chance met except in class, and were obliged to converse in mysterious asides under terror of the master's rod, that alone was enough to give to our intercourse a tone of good breeding which had no resemblance with the usual behaviour of boys to each other. I was really very much attached to them. I would have done anything they desired, and honestly believed that this feeling would last all my life.

Otherwise I was most exclusive; the rest of the school to me simply did not exist. At the same time I was beginning as it were to secrete a superficial self for social purposes, a thin outer covering which kept on good terms with every one, while my real inner self eluded them completely.

I generally contrived to sit between my two friends André and Paul; and if we were divided we exchanged constant notes in a private cypher to which we alone had the key.

Confidential on love affairs, were those notes: "I saw her to-day; she had a blue gown trimmed with grey fur, and a hat with a wing in it, etc., etc." For we each had chosen a young lady who was the usual theme of our romantic communications.

A certain infusion of such nonsense and absurdity is inevitable at this age of transition in a boy's life, and I must therefore make a note of it in passing.

In passing, too, I may say that this period lasted with me longer than with most men, because it carried me from one extreme to the other — not without striking on every reef by the way,— and I am conscious of having preserved, till I was at least five and twenty, certain strange and whimsical peculiarities.

I will now give the story of our three love affairs.

André was devoted to a young lady of sixteen at least, and already out in the world — and in his case I believe it was a genuine emotion.

The lady of my adoration was Jeanne, and no one but my two friends knew the secret. To do as they did, though it struck me as rather silly, I wrote her name in cypher on the covers of my copy books; and in a dilettante fashion, for the notion of the thing, I tried to persuade myself that I was really in love; but I must own that it was somewhat factitious, for, in point of fact the little coquetry of our first acquaintance had become, between Jeanne and me, a very true and hearty friendship — a hereditary friendship, so to speak, the reflection of that which had subsisted between our grandparents. My real first love, which I will presently relate and which also dates from that time, was for the vision of a dream.

As to Paul — it was a great shock at first, especially with the notions I then held — his passion was for a little shop-girl at a perfumer's; he saw her on his Sundays oût behind the shop window. To be sure her name was Stella, or Olympia, or something of the kind, which raised her considerably, and he took care to wrap up this love affair in a sort of ethereal and poetic sentimentality to make it acceptable. He was constantly passing up mysterious scraps of paper scribbled with honeyed rhymes in her honour, in which her name, ending in A, recurred again and again like the scent of pomatum.

In spite of my affection for him these verses made me smile with irritated pity. They were in a great degree the reason why I never, never, at any period of my life, thought of writing a line of poetry, a fact which is I believe singular, if not unique. My notes were always penned in prose, unfettered by rules, in a boldly independent style.

LXXVI.

THIS very Paul, too, knew the poems of a forbidden author, one Alfred de Musset, which troubled my soul as something unheard-of, revolting but delightful. He would whisper them to me in school in a scarcely audible murmur, and with a twinge of remorse I would make him begin again:

> Jacque était immobile et regardait Marie,
> Je ne sais ce qu'avait cette femme endormie
> D'étrange dans ses traits, de grand, de *déjà vu.*[*]

. . . .

In my brother's study, where I was wont to shut myself up from time to time, reviving my regrets at his departing, I had seen on a bookshelf a large volume of the poet's works, and I had often been tempted to take it down; but I had been told that I was never to touch one of these books without telling my parents beforehand, and my conscience always stopped me.

As to asking leave, I knew only too well that it would not be given.

---

[*] Jacque stood motionless looking at Marie;
I know not what there was in the sleeping woman
That was strange in her face, and fine, and *seen before.*

LXXVII.

THIS is a dream I had in the fourteenth May of my life. It came to me in one of those mild, soft nights which follow the long delicious twilight.

Up in my little room I had gone to sleep to the distant sound of the dance-rounds sung by the sailors and girls round the May-poles in the streets. Until I was sound asleep I had listened to those very old French refrains which the common people sing on that coast in full hearty voices, and which came up to me softened, mellowed, poetised through the tranquil stillness. I had been lulled rather weirdly by the noise of this glad life and overflowing glee, such as come, during their brief youth, to beings so much simpler than we are and less aware of death.

In my dream it was dusk, not gloomy, but as sweet as the May night outside, warm and full of the good smell of spring. I was in our back-garden which was not altered nor strange, and I walked on under the walls covered with flowering jasmine, honeysuckle and roses; but doubtful and agitated, seeking I knew not what, conscious of some one who was waiting for me and whom I longed to see, or of something unfamiliar which was going to happen and which had gone to my head by anticipation.

At a spot where a very old rose-tree grew, planted by some ancestor and reverently preserved, though it scarcely produced a single rose every two or three years, I perceived a young girl standing motionless with a mysterious smile.

The darkness grew oppressive and enervating. All round me the gloom deepened, too; but on her there was a faint gleam as if from a reflector, which defined her figure clearly against a thin line of shadow.

I felt that she must be very pretty and young; but her eyes and brow were shrouded in darkness; I could see nothing plainly but her mouth, which was parted in a smile, and the oval of her chin was lovely. She stood quite close to the old flowerless rose tree, almost among the branches. And the night grew darker and darker. She seemed quite at home there, dropped from I knew not whence, without any door having opened to admit her; she seemed to think it quite natural that she should be there, and I quite natural that I should find her there.

I went very close up to her to look at her eyes which evaded me, and then I suddenly saw them quite plainly in spite of the deepening night, which was heavier every moment. They smiled as her lips did; and they were not just any eyes, as though she had been an abstract image of youth; on the contrary, they were very particularly *somebody's* eyes; as I looked at them they came back to me as eyes I had loved and now found again, with a gush of infinite tenderness . . . .

Waking with a start, I tried to detain the vision, which faded, faded—more and more intangible and unreal as my spirit grew clearer with the effort to remember. Was it possible, after all, that she was not and had never been anything but an airy lifeless nothing, now reabsorbed into the void of imaginary, non-existent things. I tried to go to sleep and see her once more; the idea that it was all gone, nothing but a dream, was a disappointment almost to desperation.

It was very long before I forgot her; I loved her — loved her deeply; whenever I thought of her it was with great agitation, at once sweet and painful; everything that was not she, seemed to me for the time colourless and mean. I was really in love; it was truly love, with its great melancholy and its great mystery, with its sad but supreme enchantment, left clinging like a perfume to everything it has touched; that corner of the garden where she appeared to me, and the old rose-tree which had held her in its sprays, had ever after an inexplicable anguish and ecstasy that they had borrowed from her.

LXXVIII.

IT was glorious June, evening, the exquisite hour of twilight. I was alone in my brother's room; I had been there some minutes; through the window, wide open to the rosy sky shaded into gold, came the sharp cries of the house-swallows as they circled in clouds above the old roofs.

No one knew that I was there; never had I felt more utterly alone at the top of the house nor more tempted by the unknown. My heart beat high as I opened that volume of Musset: *Don Paez.*

The first melodious, musical phrases were as it were sung to me in an entrancing golden voice:

. . . .

    Sourcils noirs, blanches mains, et, pour la petitesse
    De ses pieds, elle était Andalouse et comtesse.*

. . . .

    Eyebrows black, hands white, and for the smallness
    Of her feet, she was Andalusian and a countess.

When the spring night had quite closed in, when my eyes, held very close to the page, could distinguish nothing of the magical verse but little grey lines on the white page, I went out alone into the town.

In the almost empty streets, as yet unlighted, the rows of limes and acacias in bloom scented the air and made the darkness deeper. Having pulled my felt hat over my eyes, like Don Paez, I walked on with a brisk, light step, looking up at the balconies and dreaming I know not what childish dreams of nights in Spain and Andalusian serenades.

LXXIX.

AGAIN the holidays came round; our journey to the South was made once more, for the third time; and there, under the glorious sunshine of August and September, everything went on as it had done in former years: the same games with my faithful little friends, the same excursions in the vineyards and mountains, the same reveries of mediæval times among the ruins of Castelnau, and the same zealous search along the lonely path where our veins of silver lay, with the same buccaneering airs — although the little Peyrals had really ceased to believe in the mines.

This regular recurrence of the same events each summer sometimes made me almost believe that my child-life might be indefinitely prolonged; but, meanwhile, I had ceased to have "joy on waking." A sort of uneasiness, like that which lurks in the consciousness of a task not done, came over me every morning with increasing pangs at the thought that time was flying, that the holidays were coming to an end, and that I had not yet found courage to seal my fate.

LXXX.

AND one day, when mid-September was already past, I perceived, from the pressing anxiety which weighed on me at waking, that

I could evade it no longer. The term I had fixed for myself had come.

As to the decision, it was already more than half formed in the depths of my mind; to make it effective, I had now only to announce it, and I vowed that the day should not pass without its being done and done bravely. It was to my brother that I first would declare it, fancying that he, too, would do his utmost to oppose my scheme, but in the end he would take my part and help me to gain my point.

So after our mid-day dinner, when the sun was at the fiercest, I carried my paper and pen into my uncle's garden and there locked myself in to write my letter. It was one of my habits as a child to do my lessons or write letters in the open air, often in the oddest places — among the boughs of a tree or on a roof.

It was a scorching and cloudless autumn day, quiet to sadness in that old garden which seemed more silent — more foreign, perhaps, than ever, impressing me with more than common regret at being away from my mother, and seeing the summer end so far from home and from the flowers in my own dear little garden. But, after all, what I had come here to write would result in my being more than ever parted from all I loved so well, and it put me in a mournful mood. I felt as though there were actually something solemn in the atmosphere of that garden; as though the very walls, the plum-trees, the trellised vines, the fields of luzerne beyond, had an interest in this first serious step in my life which was about to be taken in their sight.

I hesitated which of three places I should sit in to write, all three boiling hot, with very little shade. It was a mere excuse for gaining time and delaying this letter, which, according to the views I then held, would make my decision irrevocable when once I had thus proclaimed it. The earth was already strewn with russet vine-trails and dead leaves; hollyhocks and dahlias, grown as tall as trees, had a few sparse blossoms at the top of their straggling stems; the torrid sun was finishing the ripening of those large-seeded, yellow grapes with a musky flavour, which are always later than the others, and, in spite of the intense heat and the translucent blue sky, there was a sense of ended summer in the air.

I finally settled myself in the arbour at the bottom of the garden; the vines had lost most of their leaves; but the last metallic-blue butterflies were still to be seen, and the wasps haunting the muscat grapes.

And there, in calm, still loneliness, in the summer silence full of insect-music, I wrote and timidly signed my compact with the sea.

Of the letter itself I remember not a word; but I well remember the emotion of sealing it, as if, with that envelope, I had sealed my fate for ever.

After another short pause for thought, I wrote the address; my brother's name and that of a land in the furthest East, where he then was.—Now there was nothing more to be done but to carry it the post-office; but I remained sitting there a long time, very thoughtful, with my back against the heated wall where the lizards were scampering, and nursing on my knees, with a sense of woe, the little square of paper on which I had signed away my future life. Then, having a fancy to look out at the horizon and get a sight of space, I put my foot in the well-known hole by which I climbed to watch the escape of the butterflies I had failed to catch, and hoisted myself to the top of the wall where I rested on my elbows. I saw the same familiar distance, the hills draped in reddening vines, the mountains where the trees were turning yellow and shedding their leaves, and far away the great stone ruin of Castelnau. In front of all this lay Bories, with its old arched gateway, and, as I saw it, the plaintive air: *"Ah! ah! la bonne histoire!"* came back to me in a strange voice, and the sulphur butterfly, which had been lying there two years with a pin through it, under glass in my little museum.

It was near the hour when the old country mail coach would be starting, carrying away the letters. I got down from my wall, I quitted the old garden, locking it behind me, and slowly made my way to the post-office.

I walked on like a being in a dream, paying no heed to anything or anybody. My mind was wandering far: in the fern-forests of the Delightful Isle, over the sands of gloomy Senegal, where that uncle had been who owned the museum, and across the great Southern Ocean, where there were shoals of flying-fish.

The positive and proximate certainty of seeing all this intoxicated me; for the first time in all my life the world seemed to lie open before me; a new light shone on my path—a rather sorrowful light, it is true, and rather lonely, but powerful, and piercing to the uttermost horizon of old age and death.

Certain very childish fancies intruded themselves now and then on this vast daydream. I saw myself in a sailor's uniform, walking in the sunshine on the burning shore of some tropical town, or coming home after perilous voyages; bringing with me sea-chests full of wonderful things, out of which the cockroaches would creep as in the yard at Jeanne's house when her father's cases were unpacked.

And suddenly my heart was very full. These home-comings after long travel could not yet take place for many years—and then the faces that would welcome me would be changed by time.—I pictured them at once, those well-beloved faces; I saw them all together in a dim vision—a group which hailed me with smiles of loving welcome, but which was so sad to contemplate! Wrinkles on every brow; and my mother with white curls as she has at this day.—And my grandaunt Bertha, so old already, would she still be there?

I was hastily and fearfully calculating my grandaunt's age, when I reached the post-office. But I did not hesitate; my hand only trembled a little as I dropped my letter into the box, and the die was cast.

LXXXI.

HERE end these reminiscences; in the first place because succeeding events are not yet far enough away from me to be laid before unknown readers; and also because I think that my childhood really ended on the day when I thus decided my lot.

I was then fourteen and a half; I had three years before me to prepare to enter the naval school, so it was altogether a reasonable and possible plan.

I had, however, to come into collision with refusals and difficulties of every kind before I found myself entered on the *Borda*. After that I had to live through many years of hesitancy, struggles and mistakes, many a hill of penance to climb. I had to pay cruelly for my early life as a sensitive little recluse; to reforge and harden both my physical and moral temper by sheer force of will; — till, one day, when I was about seven-and-twenty, a circus manager, having seen how my muscles now acted like steel springs, expressed his admiration in these words, the truest I ever heard spoken: "What a pity, Monsieur, that your training began so late!"

LXXXII.

. . . .

MY sister and I expected to go back next summer again to that village in the south. But Azraël crossed our path; terrible and unforeseen events devastated our peaceful, happy home-life.

It was not till fifteen years later, after having scoured the seas, that I once more beheld that nook of France.

Everything was changed; the uncle and aunt slept in the graveyard; the sons were scattered; the daughter, who already had threads of silver in her hair, was about to leave the place and the empty house where she could not bear to live alone, never to return. Titi and Màricette —who had lost these baby-names—were tall girls in mourning whom I should not have recognized.

Between two voyages, in a hurry as usual, my life rushing on its feverish course, I came back for only a few hours on a pilgrimage of memories, wishing to see the house where "my uncle in the South" had lived, before it was given over to strange hands.

It was November; a cold grey sky had entirely altered the aspect of the country, which I had never before seen but under the splendid summer sun.

After spending the only morning I had to spare in seeing everything once more, with ever-growing melancholy, under the winter clouds, I found I had forgotten the old garden and the vine-grown arbour, where my life's fortune had been decided, and I would wish to visit it at the last moment, before the carriage started which was to bear me away for ever.

"Go alone," said my cousin; she, too, busied in closing her trunks; and she gave me the big key—the very same big key which I had been wont to carry when I went there butterfly-hunting, net in hand, in the glowing and glorious days gone by. Those summers of my childhood, how wonderful and full of enchantment they had been.

So for the very last time I went into the garden, which struck me at first as having grown smaller under the dull sky. I went straight to the arbour, now bare of leaves and desolate, where I had written the all-important letter to my brother, and by the help of the same hole in the wall I hoisted myself to the top, to steal a glance at the surrounding country and hastily bid it a last farewell; then I saw Bories, looking strangely near and very small, too; unrecognizable—as indeed the mountains were in the distance, as if they had settled down into little hills. And the whole scene, which I had seen of old in the sunshine, was dreary now in the dull grey light. I felt as though the last autumn of my life were upon me, as it was on the earth.

And the world itself—the world I had thought of as so immense, so full of delightful amazements on the day when I had looked over this wall after making my decision — was not this whole world shrunken and faded in my eyes, like this poor little landscape.

The sight more especially of the gate of Bories, like a ghost of itself under the wintry sky, filled me with infinite melancholy.

As I looked at it I was reminded of the sulphur butterfly, still in its glass case in my little museum; still in the same spot, with its hues as fresh as ever, while I had been sailing on every sea. For many years I had forgotten the association of the two things; and then, as the yellow butterfly recurred to my mind, recalled by the gate of Bories, I heard in my brain a piping voice, singing quite softly: *"Ah! ah! la bonne histoire!"* The voice was strange and thin, but above all sad — sad enough for tears, sad enough to sing over a grave the song of vanished years and long dead summers.

THE END.

ADVERTISEMENTS

RARAHU; OR THE MARRIAGE OF LOTI.—By **Pierre Loti**, from the French by Mrs. Clara Bell. *Authorized edition*. One volume. 16mo. paper, 50 cts. 12mo. cloth, $1.00.

Not long ago we had occasion to speak of Julien Viand's "Pêcheur d'Island"—that wonderful romance of the wild and frozen North in which marvellous descriptions of sea-faring life in Icelandic waters were intermingled with equally marvellous pages depicting the progress of a love affair between a wild young mariner and a beautiful daughter of Brittany. In the "Mariage de Loti," now translated by Clara Bell under the title of *Rarahu*, we are taken to the antipodes and the author lavishes all his power as a writer in painting in the most exquisite and idyllic colors the experiences of a young naval officer during a six months' stay at Tahiti. Tahitian customs are not based on Puritanic ideals, and this marriage of Loti would be regarded as something far different under less benignant conditions; but morals, like religion, are, as we all know, largely a matter of geographical location, and of this affair between the foreigner and the pearl of Papeete it may at least be said that it reflected the utmost devotion while it endured. The book is chiefly remarkable for its exotic flavor; it breathes the true atmosphere of the tropics. Tahiti, as Julien Viaud reveals that far-distant island, is a paradise of the senses, a veritable abode of syrens for those who go down to the sea in ships, and all its remote and unfamiliar charm,—the brooding silences of nature, the vast forests haunted neither by singing bird or venomous insect, the towering peaks, the ever-flowing cataracts leaping from the heights, the cool pools of refreshing water, the tremendous surf rolling in forever on the resistant shore, the gorgeous semi-civilization of Pomaré's court, the existence of a simple-minded, imaginative people who find their wants amply provided for by nature and who pass their hours with no thought or care for the morrow—all this gets a place in Julien Viaud's book. As for Rarahu she is a tropical flower born to dazzle for a time with her beauty and to intoxicate the soul with her adorable fancies, only to fade at last into something worse than death. This is Tahiti seen with the eyes of the poet, pictured by one who chooses his colors deftly and who has no call to portray the dreary or the commonplace. The book as it stands is a masterpiece of art, a symphony in words, expressing with graceful and often poignant modulation the emotions that stir the heart at twenty and make existence a vista of perpetual pleasure or a bourn of limitless despair. Viaud is one who at least in fancy has sounded all the heights and depths of passion, and yet there is in his method a reserve which piques interest. Being a genuine artist he knows with unerring felicity when and at what point to stay his hand. — *The Beacon, Boston, July* 26, 1890.

FROM LANDS OF EXILE.—By Pierre Loti, from the French by Clara Bell, in one vol. Paper, 50 cts. Cloth, 90 cts.

"THE FRENCH have a knack for dedications. The other day we had occasion to notice Balzac's 'Modeste Mignon,' to which was prefixed one of the most beautiful dedications we had ever read: short, pregnant, eloquent, compressing in a single paragraph — but a paragraph of which Balzac alone is master — the concentrated adoration of a life-time. Pierre Loti, in this volume of charming translations, shows himself hardly less skilful in his introductory note, as he presents to us a brief memoir of the inspirer and inspiration of some of his best work — Mrs. Edward Lee Childe, 'whose never-to-be-forgotten image rises before me, strangely vivid, whenever I have time to think.' Between Loti and this delicate, gifted Parisienne there existed sympathies of which we have prescience and foreshadowing in these marvellous sketches, — an Andromeda chained to a sofa in the Champs Elysées while Perseus ran the Eastern seas, revelled in their gorgeous coloring, and brought back from them — 'seas of exile'— impressions of the most exquisite vividness. There is true Orientalism in this book. Fragmentary as its reminiscences are, they are yellow with China, green with Singapore, glowing with Aden, penetrated with the languor and intoxication of Annam and Far India, tremulous with palms, grotesque with uprisen memories of pagoda and Buddha-worship. An officer on a French man-of-war in the Franco-Chinese war, Loti availed himself of his opportunities, and drank in that golden, stagnant, inverted sort of Chinese life which was afforded by Cochin China and its fantastic existence. His note-book is a net with which he captured butterflies, harvested impressions, wove the East into his cocoon-hammock, and then hatched it out for us in this argentiferous form. A writer who writes mother-of-pearl, who thinks opal, who 'tools' his thought into all sorts of precious forms, and who calls his strange spoil, 'From Lands of Exile;' such is this French officer, who is at the same time a great word-artist. He is certainly endowed with the 'fruitful river of the eye,' with a retina of rare sensitiveness, with a sense of vision that dilates your own almost to pain; what he sees you see twice over : for yourself and through him. China has passed through many rarely gifted psychological organizations ; but it has never before emerged so itself, so prismatic, so alive as a chameleon is alive, with its great yellow goblinlike picturesqueness."—*The Critic.*

AN ICELAND FISHERMAN, (*Pecheur d'Islande*) A Story of Love on Land and Sea, by **Pierre Loti,** from the French by Clara Cardiot. One Volume. 16mo, Paper, 25 cents. 12mo. Cloth, 75 cents.

"'An Iceland Fisherman' is a sad but wonderfully sweet story that established on a firm foundation the reputation of its talented author almost immediately upon its publication. Breton life is painted with a masterly hand, and the fine descriptions, tenderness and pathos of the story give it an interest for all classes of cultivated readers that can never wane."—*Boston Commonwealth.*

THE COURT OF CHARLES IV. a Romance, by **B. Perez Galdós,** from the Spanish by Clara Bell, in one vol. Price, paper, 50 cts. Cloth, 90 cts.

"To this house the American reading public owes many new and delightful sensations. It has brought into popularity here a number of authors of undoubted genius whose remarkable works have been strangely overlooked by other publishers. One of this brilliant company is B. Perez Galdós, the Spanish romancer, whose 'Gloria' has recently made a profound impression in its English version at the hands of the accomplished linguist, Clara Bell. From the same author and the same translator we now receive a novel of love and war as powerful of its kind as Tolstoï's books which cover a similar range of human interest. The action takes place in the early part of this century, when Napoleon was the disturbing element of the universe. The characters who move through the thrilling pages are princes, princesses, grandees of all grades, generals and statesmen. They are mostly historical. Spanish scenery, climate, customs and manners are described with scrupulous fidelity. To read the book is like living in Spain during the eventful era to which the story is confined. As the Spanish peninsula is but little visited by American tourists, and as the 'Court of Charles IV.,' with its ambitions and intrigues, is a subject quite fresh to novelists, it follows that the present work will be eagerly bought and greatly enjoyed by all who love to explore new fields."—*The Journal of Commerce.*

CPSIA information can be obtained
at www.ICGtesting.com
Printed in the USA
BVHW040804100420
577297BV00014B/495